FEAR ICONS

21ST CENTURY ESSAYS
David Lazar and Patrick Madden, Series Editors

FEAR ICONS

ESSAYS

Kisha Lewellyn Schlegel

MAD CREEK BOOKS, AN IMPRINT OF
THE OHIO STATE UNIVERSITY PRESS
COLUMBUS

Library of Congress Cataloging-in-Publication Data
Names: Schlegel, Kisha Lewellyn, author.
Title: Fear icons : essays / Kisha Lewellyn Schlegel.
Other titles: 21st century essays.
Description: Columbus : Mad Creek Books, an imprint of The Ohio
    State University Press, [2018] | Series: 21st century essays | Includes
    bibliographical references and index.
Identifiers: LCCN 2018013921 | ISBN 9780814254943 (pbk. ; alk. paper)
Subjects: LCSH: American essays—21st century.
Classification: LCC PS3619.C4235 A6 2018 | DDC 814/.6—dc23
LC record available at https://lccn.loc.gov/2018013921

Cover design by Nathan Putens
Text design by Juliet Williams
Type set in Janson
Published by The Ohio State University Press

♾ The paper used in this publication meets the minimum requirements of the
American National Standard for Information Sciences—Permanence of Paper for
Printed Library Materials. ANSI Z39.48-1992.

CONTENTS

JESUS?

A PROLOGUE

Jesus?
    Is that you?
    In my bones?
    In my head?
    In my hand and elbow?
    Is that you in my dress?
    In my face?
    After twenty years without church, why do I think of you?
    Childhood crush?
    Because my preacher of a granddad taught me yours is the face of love?
    If you aren't really here, are you here?
    I'm gonna close my eyes.
    I'm gonna see something when nothing is there.
    When I close my eyes, I'm in the church of reproduction: Color copy Jesus; Blue eyed; Blue sky. 1985. It's Sunday school everywhere.
    "Who is Jesus?" the teacher asked.
    "The Son of God," said a boy.
    "Love," said a girl.

"A guy?" I asked.

What was wrong with me?

Did I have bees in my bonnet?

Why wasn't I a good girl who got it?

Why wasn't I like the worshippers John Berger saw in the old churches of his 1972 video *Ways of Seeing*? They believed that ". . . everything around an image is part of its meaning . . . everything around it confirms and consolidates its meaning. The extreme example is the icon. Worshippers converge upon it. Behind its image is God. Before it, believers close their eyes. They do not need to go on looking at it. They know that it marks the place of meaning."

"Sure," the Sunday school teacher nodded, "he's a 'guy.' But . . ." She stopped blinking. Eye contact was important for the point she was about to make. "He was *the* 'guy' to save *all* 'guys.'" She used the familiar term to transform my understanding of it. Isn't that what a teacher does? And an icon too?

She held up a picture of Jesus' face. "Just look into this 'guy's' eyes."

I tried to do as I was told. I looked into your eyes.

You looked like you were pretending to be brave. You looked lonely.

"See?" she said. "He's at peace."

Wait. I thought. Peace? How was she seeing *that*?

What was she looking at?

Why did she need to tell us what to see?

"Understand," she said. "God so loved the world that he gave his only son."

"What kind of love is that?" I asked.

And what was my biggest mistake?

That I couldn't believe as she did?

That I disrupted her certainty?

Or that I wanted to?

Did I love my questions more than the answer?

Did I even want an answer?

Wasn't I just annoying?

Wasn't I just sassing the teacher? (A volunteer!)

She only wanted to show me the light of Jesus' face.
Blue sky.
Blue-eyed.
Why are you always so white?
"Out," she said. "Out!"
How long did I sit on the linoleum floor of that empty hallway?
Were the lights really off?
Did I feel injustice?
Or confirmation?
I feared my teacher. Her belief worked by limiting mine.
This implicit understanding felt like my companion.
Was it actually You?
Jesus?
Who am I asking these questions to?
Who is this you?
Me?
Farther in? [Bromwich and Bevis]
Or the you I read?
The you who reads me?
Is this my trinity?
The you, you, and the Holy you of reading?
We, reading, make a circuit.
Of connection?
Of judgment?
Breaker, breaker.
Do you read me?
What happens when we read someone?
Why do questions pile up like bailiffs, asks Tomaž Šalamun. I put the poet's name in the brackets of my lungs: [*Tomaž Šalamun*]. He's so much freer than me and not just because he's dead. He lives in translation—which is a motion between languages.

I only speak English, but I don't feel at home in its syntax. Sometimes I make marks on the page that only you could read out of generosity or love. I make mistakes that reveal me. I write site instead of sight. (Because I'm located but not seeing?) I confuse scarred with scared. The spelling. And the meaning? The single r that distinguishes them drops in and out; don't they have suffering in common?

I know I've abandoned the logic that might make us friends. (Intro, support, support, support, conclusion.) I used to love that five-paragraph shit! I wanted so badly to prove what I knew. But the formula never revealed much. The short containers called paragraphs, so easy to order, were little coffins in the ground.

I died in that form and came back a question mark.

Here's my argument. I have eyes I try to keep open. It hurts.

Is this how I make myself vulnerable?

I ask your established face—you "icon of the invisible God, the firstborn over all creation," (Col 1:15):

Is this the way I pray?

Is this how I learned the religion that is mine—the religion of persistent looking, which is the ritual of language?

Of asking?

"What do you see?" asked the teacher.

"God!" said a boy.

"Love," said a girl.

Suffering, I say.

Why must you carry it?

In your arms?

Your body?

Your face?

Does your pain distract us from our fears?

Of death and the greater fear of our own pain?

Why does one person's suffering make another feel safe?

Am I there yet?

At the question?

Who are we to each other when we're afraid?

BIN LADEN

Just outside of a town called New Hope, a woman takes aim at a bearded man. He holds a rifle, but it's his face that's a grenade in the brain: the chipper gaze, the full mouth, the jaw curved like a coffin. The woman burrows into a gun. Her eye disappears behind its sights.

Like all the other participants, she has paid $162 to reenact the death of Osama bin Laden, recently killed by Navy SEALs who stormed his bedroom on a moonless night. She has come for the violent relief that refused to stay. She's come to kill a man who's already dead.

The Navy SEAL standing behind her will teach her how. "If you don't train and don't know what to do," he tells her, "it's deer in the headlights time!"

In this shooting gallery called "SEALed Mindset," there is no time. He's already here, in the building, hiding in a room staged to look like the one where he died. The man in a fake beard, white turban, and robe really is him. He's just around the corner. He sits on the edge of a bed, waiting for her to open the door.

"The icon is a door," said Saint Stephen the Younger (before he died for the icon in 767). It opens to salvation. It can take you across the threshold of this life and into that eternal one where suffering is a memory.

To glimpse God, believers in the ornate sanctuaries of some churches sit in flickering candlelight and pray to a large screen of icons, called the iconostasis. It stands between the main body of the church, where believers pray for lost keys and children alike, and the hidden altar, where unseen clergy turn bread into the body and blood into salvation.

In the iconostasis, Mary is to the left of center and the Savior to the right. Between them, an angel tells a cowering Mary that she will bear a son. "Fear not, Mary!" he says, even though, just a few panels over, Jesus hangs from his cross. St. John holds up a baptizing hand, affirming the meaning of loss: "You are made new!" Death is salvation. But only for those who believe. The final cross is only the beginning for those who know how to look. For them, the holy voices sing, "Rejoice! O, Full of Grace! The Lord is with you!" When he first made man, God cried out *Eikon!* Likeness! Every face in the iconostasis is the face of a person who walked this earth and suffered and died and yet, here they are. Loving you.

For those who believe, the icon is not a barrier. It is a door made of flesh.

It's a body whose shadow is God. Its shadow text is the Bible: *Therefore, brethren, enter the sanctuary by the blood of Jesus, by the new and living way which he opened for us through the curtain, that is, through his flesh. [Hebrews]*

His flesh opens.

The only thing more frightening is the possibility that it won't.

———————

The light is dim in the shooting gallery. A perpetual dusk seems to have settled inside. Not the nuanced light of shadows, but a kind of ash light. The wall meets the ceiling without a discernible edge. The hand is the gun that it holds.

She pulls the trigger.

The bright pop of her gun rips a dark hole in the fabric. She can still see his face in front of her. He's there. Standing. She shoots again and again until the target falls. He's gone, but the idea of him still hangs in the air.

She maintains her position.

She's ready.

The instructor touches her shoulder. He hands her a paint gun made to look like a real gun. He guides her toward the "Live Scenario Room." She wears night goggles. The ability to see so well in the dark makes the light intolerable. She walks down a hallway lit by a fluorescence so bright she can't see.

———

I was raised on God in a church without icons. We prayed in a sanctuary of stained glass made only of pastel-colored squares. The windows held none of the usual images of revelation. We used words to see Jesus. We spoke of the blood and the body as we took communion each week in that church in downtown Decatur, Georgia. Words turned the unleavened bread between our fingers into the body of God in our mouths. "This is my body, broken for you," everyone prayed. They drank the juice, pretending it was blood. I imagined it sweating out of their skin, covering them with protection. I imagined salvation dresses made out of blood.

After breaking the body, they turned to each other and said, "Good morning. Peace be with you," even as a small pool of red juice remained in the emptied plastic cups we passed between us, stained with a blood-light that shined its clear message onto us: This is the only way you won't die.

The pierced foot. The slaughtered lamb. I was taught to read these images with love. But I feared the belief they required. Their blood. Their likeness. I couldn't receive the wound as a form of love. There was a wound. I didn't believe in that kind of sacrifice. I didn't believe anyone's death would save me.

I sat at the edge of every pew. I read the bible only when I was told to. I sang only when I stood next to my retired preacher of a granddad who passed his hymnal to me if ever I was quiet and reminded me to sing. I loved him. I sang the words that held no meaning for me because they held meaning for him. He passed the communion tray, and when he turned his head to pray, I held my hand over the unleavened bread called the body and the grape juice called blood and took nothing. I passed the tray, silver and heavy with a weight I refused to hold.

I turned away from the people around me who held their belief like a beloved and toward the stained glass that rose to an untouchable height. Each pane filled with variable light. The clouds formed shadows. Lightning flashed surprise without thunder. The clouds passed on. Summer again drove her searing light through the glass, revealing that every lit-up square of pastel was edged by the heavy lead needed to hold it safely in place.

The lead was slightly puckered in places where two pieces had been soldered together. They undulated like the varicose veins that run behind the knees of women in my family, swollen and tortuously lengthened—the kind of veins that always look painful and yet the women walk on.

These were the women who made me and whom I loved and relied on for my life. In their bodies lived suffering in its complexity. Its actuality.

Here was the image I knew to hold the complications of this life. The blood in the light.

In the edges, I found a way to keep looking.

A door clicks open.

The man dressed in a fake beard and turban throws up his hands as the woman finds the trigger. Just before she squeezes it with her whole hand, as she was taught to do, just before the cold bullet goes hot through the air at 3,200 feet per second, there is a pause, tiny and inconceivable.

Along this edge of time, the heart beats faster, at a clip usually reserved for those who are running. But no one is running. The body is still but not at rest. This is fear. Fleshy. Like a body, pressing against another body with purpose, its function to protect us, as it did our ancestors, from poisonous snakes and great heights even as we walked toward them, filled with the strange desire to take a step closer and, having never died, test our tacit belief in invincibility.

The body feels fear in the made-up room and the real one, as described in the *Abbottabad Commission Report* of 2013. The Navy SEALs blew open the steel doors to find bin Laden's children and grandchildren huddled in the corners of the stairwell. The children's hands rose like fireworks. They sang the prayer "Lâ ilâha illa Allâh." "There is no god but The God."

The Navy SEALs entered the upstairs bedroom. The gun kicked back into the shoulder of the one who pulled the trigger, as he was trained to do, believing violence is a form of safety, the way I do when I'm alone in bed at night and hear every creak of the house as an intruder who comes so close that I imagine the brass lamp is a weapon I'll use to bash in his skull as if I know how or could.

I'm not a believer in icons. I am their child.

From a young age, I leaned into the television screen, toward the faces I loved: My A-Team. My Huxtables. My Winnie Cooper. My iconostasis. I won't describe them. Their noses and eyes, their faces didn't make them my icons—it was their essence and the context in which I read this essence.

Just beside the frame of the television was a framed photo of my dad, who died when I was five. It was a professional portrait kept there for proof of existence. To make it resonate like revelation, my dad sat in front of a fake cloud. Angelic. In a suit. Here was a dad I was told was mine. Here was the man who I knew to have moved and been alive and could not remember as alive.

Sometimes I had a staring contest with him. I waited for him to blink, as if the still image were a pause in the recording of our lives, a glitch in the playback. I had the sense that inside of that frame, just beyond his shoulder, was the life I had lived with him but didn't know. In that former world, he looked at me. He recognized me as his own. He spoke with a voice I couldn't remember but must have known and so must still have, deep inside this body, resonating into now even though I hear nothing. I stared, only to be returned to the moment when I stood by his black casket and saw my reflection in the gloss of its surface. Five years old. Hands slack against my skirt. Eyes fixed. Face stiff. Not crying. Never crying. Looking at myself in a mirror made by his death. Waiting.

In my living room, I returned to his photograph to connect to the life hidden within. I wanted to see it as much as I feared I might. I couldn't look at the photo for too long. At any moment, my dad might blink at me. He might turn his almond-shaped eyes on my almond-shaped eyes, and I would hear him without hearing his voice. I would hear him say what I already believed: *You will never understand anything.*

———————

The man in a fake beard and turban rushes at the woman. She raises her gun full of paint pellets, so red and bright, aiming, as she has been taught to do, at the white robe over the man's heart.

The woman pulls the trigger; the man plays dead under her paint. He stays on the ground, dressed in blood.

She turns to the camera.

"What a rush!" she says. "I'm sweating!" She gives the former Navy SEAL a high five.

I stop the Internet footage of her from the nightly news. Violence illuminates her face with joy. Hers are the glittering eyes of the crowds that ran into the night when they learned bin Laden was dead. They drank beer and climbed light poles and held signs of bin Laden's face with "Osama bin gotten" written in red across his eyes. The college kids cried "USA! USA!" until their faces were wet with relief.

The night seemed to collapse onto itself. The people celebrated death until all of the sturdy cameras shook and so everything shook: the trees, the grass, the fields, all life, the brain inside each head, and the little brain inside of each heart. There was no room to think or feel. There was no room for me. Afraid, I blinked like a cursor.

I did what I do now. I make myself as comfortable as possible. I watch my imagination. It comes most alive when I'm in the dark of my own house. I go to bed in the quiet only to hear something scratching at the sheetrock, crawling between the walls of the rooms I inhabit. Every muscle tightens until I ache with the desire to burn it all down. Only when morning comes and light exposes the walls to be stable do I tell myself that I want to know what's inside. Only then do I want a sledgehammer to open up those walls and make way for a flashlight. I want to look into the eyes shining back at me.

The woman's face fills my screen. Her blister eyes. Her freckles.

It's Saturday, in the middle of summer. I could be in a park somewhere, listening to birds. I could be at home with my son who's not yet two. But I haven't left this room all day. I drink stale coffee with cream. I hide in a room without windows or fresh air, hoping to see something more than I see. Her white skin. Ligaments. Threads of eyelashes. The warp they cause. The buckle of experience reenacted.

Freckles spread across her cheekbones and down the delicate bridge of her nose, and I refuse to think of the sunny childhood days that put them there. Her freckles are the color of dried blood to me.

I should stop. Turn away. Go for a walk. Out in the world are birds and beetles, grass and ferns so delicate that some are called maidenhair.

I go nowhere. I rewind this footage, returning to the screen. I flit about her face, another moth to the flame.

Another metaphor.

The icon is a metaphor that used to be a person.

"How skinny he was," the Navy SEAL who claims to have killed bin Laden told *Esquire* magazine. "As I watched him breathe out the last part of air, I thought: Is this the best thing I've ever done, or the worst thing I've ever done?" It was then that he looked along the edge of the room and discovered he wasn't alone. "Bin Laden's youngest son, who is about two or three, was standing there on the other side of the bed. I didn't want to hurt him because I'm not a savage. There was a lot of screaming. He was crying. Just in shock. I didn't like that he was scared. He's a kid and had nothing to do with this. I picked him up. I put some water on his face."

In a news clipping, the boy has a dimple on his chin, right in the center. Or maybe it's a small cut. The image is grainy. It's hard to see his face. It is impossible to forget. He was three years old when he watched his father die. His name is Hussein bin Laden.

It's always this way. Death returns me to the living people who must survive it. And suffer.

When I look at the woman again, I'm thinking of Hussein bin Laden. Her celebration of death becomes a celebration of his suffering. Her glee an explosion. *The victors' eyes become live shells* in me. [*Adnan*] I find myself locating the small space between her eyes—that pale square of skin. White. Vulnerable. The edges of her face dissolve into this single target. It's all I see. A reduction. With the paint gun in my mind, I blow her mind into correction.

I'm in the thicket now, even though all is quiet in my world. So quiet. But look how the planes still crash inside. She's busy with her hurt, and I'm busy with mine. I return to her face as she returns to bin Laden's as we return to the grief that lives on inside and will never die. We want to destroy that which destroys. The pain we make of this life. This country. America.

I circle that word. I circle all the words that claim to comfort only to lay claim.

I circle myself.

I claim to want to love. To seek that which might take me beyond the wound—beyond the desire to wound. And yet, I don't want to see this woman's face.

She has a name, and I don't want to know it.

She has beliefs; I have no questions for her.

I make of her another thing to fear.

Or is this hate?

I don't know.

I feel like I'm making a dress out of blood.

MOTHER MARY

Mary is luminous with worry as Jesus stretches his baby-arm across her chest. Made from tempera paint, her skin glows like the egg she is—that fertile source of Jesus, who promised to feed us all. And yet, the light doesn't quite reach her eyes in this icon from twelfth-century Russia. She peers out from a black mantle edged in gold ribbon. A gold, eight-pointed star hangs over her heart. Another dangles over her forehead. No matter where she looks, the star she bore is never far from view.

The child looks at his mother in this color reproduction I ordered from Russia and hung on my wall. He looks at her and she looks into my living room where I watch my son learn to walk. In the cross-gaze, we are all secretly looking within.

I worry my son will fall. My son holds onto the couch and grabs for the laundry basket. He misses, but he doesn't fall. He looks ahead. I look to Mary, who has the look of a friend and not an icon called the *Virgin of Vladimir*, the *Vladimirskaya*, made by someone called a "writer," and not a "painter."

The writer of the *Vladimirskaya* made her according to tradition. He chose a hardwood like linden or birch and connected the wood with dovetail and butterfly joints. He boiled animal skin and bones into the glue that could hold linen to wood. He added eight coats of thin gesso. After it cured for a few months or a year, he drew her image in charcoal. He used a compass to draw the halos. He mixed colors of cinnabar and verdigris and painted in a progression from dark tones to light. He began with the background, followed by the garments and finally the flesh of hands and faces that he gilded in gold and silver and burnished with a wolf canine mounted on a stick. He didn't sign his name; according to tradition, the human maker doesn't exist once an icon is complete. But he didn't hide. He wrote her face with feeling. He did what few if any had ever done before: he imagined the mother in Mary. Unlike all the other Marys who came before this one, he did not give the *Vladimirskaya* the simplified gaze of a stoic. He gave her a gaze like the firm pressure applied to a wound.

Gentle and firm, the expression on her face caused the Greeks to call her *Eleousa*, for compassion, and the Russians, *Umilenie*, for tender emotion. And it's true. Her gaze is compassionate *and* tender. But her eyes are scooped-out earth. She knows the death she holds. She has seen the tomb. She's tender alright. But she is tender *through* suffering. She's a mother, marked by the endless love that invites endless fears.

I look to her and just as quickly look away. She is so real to me. My neck burns with recognition. When I see her, I don't think: God and the Virgin. I think: woman, child. I think that Jesus wears a yellow striped outfit that I would buy for my son if I could find it online. I think skin. I think, Mary, Mary, quite contrary, what people make of you: white, black, happy, sad, gilded in gold or pearls, the milk-giver, the silent virgin, intercessor. We call you vessel and forget you were human. We forget you were sixteen. A mother. Afraid.

Afraid, we call on our mother. Mother!

Soldiers once brought coins of your face into battle and called you "Guard," and "General," "invincible ally." Stalin might have turned churches into urinals, but he kept the original *Vladimirskaya*. As the Germans attacked Moscow, he might even have put this version of you on a plane that circled the city, believing that keeping you safe would make the Germans retreat.

More recently, a man walked into the Brooklyn Museum and approached a six-foot-tall Chris Ofili painting called *The Holy Virgin Mary*. In this version of you, you float on a blistering gold background. A colorful dress flaps open to reveal a single breast, its nipple sculpted in 3-D out of elephant dung. Around you are images that, from a distance, look like sets of lungs that want to be butterflies. Up close, it's clear that the butterflies are women's bottoms and vaginas, spread open and dislocated from their bodies, exposed and exploited—here is my body, a vessel for you—an obscenity so honest that it renders a tender and revelatory rawness in me. But not the man. The man passed the museum guards and pulled a tube of white paint from his coat. He squeezed out its milk and smeared it over your face and breasts. A nearby guard called out, "It's not the Virgin Mary. It's a painting!" The man kept spreading his paint with his hands as if pulling a sheet over his naked mother. He covered your body as if this would protect him from your real and suffering love.

He had his idea of you, and I suppose I have mine. We aren't so different from the men who scraped the walls of caves, believing the white powder that came off was the milk you left behind. They put the powder in vials and mixed it with water and drank it for protection and said Mary. Mary, a name that means plump. Sweet. Dumpling. Or just as easily means wished for a child. Bitter sea. Rebelliousness.

––––––––––––

When I was pregnant, my body was a bulbous symbol that strangers interpreted. They walked up to me in public places and strapped their hands to my private belly. One woman told me I would have a girl. Another told me not to worry; the baby would come out one way or another.

Unlike the strangers around me, I didn't know what to make of this body that was mine and not mine. My body moved through the world of other people without me, and it grew without me. I watched my belly round into a question mark.

I told myself I could handle labor. I listened hard to the yogi on the DVD when she said, "Labor is a sensation, not pain." She had me hold my arms straight out, away from my body for three minutes. She said that when the pressure became too much, I needed to tell myself, "I just started. I just put my arms into the air. Look at them. There they are."

I was good at it. I told myself my arms weren't part of my body. But that wasn't her point. She wanted me to pay attention to the sensation, not ignore it. She wanted me to feel it and by feeling it, know I could survive it.

I had no trouble calling the first contractions "sensations." They came while I napped off and on through the night. When I couldn't sleep anymore, I walked around the 2 a.m. neighborhood with my husband and doula. We passed between trees thick with new leaves, opening like mouths. "Move a bit faster," my doula said. Faster. The contractions came and went like rushed hurricanes. They washed into me, pounding and breaking, until I was throwing up yellow bile. This was not sensation. It was obliteration. I did not eat or rest. I stood without sleeping for twenty-four hours. I stood next to a bed. Between contractions, I lowered my head onto the mattress and disappeared.

Images from my past came to me or I went to them. I didn't imagine. I actually held a white flower. A boy I loved but couldn't name said something I couldn't understand. Voices bent through me and into me. My body was a parenthesis. Everything human seemed suddenly to be.

When the pain returned, I tried to tell myself, I've just started. I've never done this before. But the pain returned so quickly, with or without me, that I finally heard myself say out loud, "I can't do this."

My doula put her face up to my face, so that it was all I could see. "You *are* doing it," she said. "This is it."

I returned to a tub of warm water in a dark room. The pain came. I fell into it. Dark and enclosed—I was *a well staring at the sky*. [*Pessoa*]

A nurse asked, "Are you pushing?"

"Pushing," I said to no one.

"She's pushing," she said. Her voice sifted through me along with all the other voices that came and went. She brought me back to the bed, where the only stable thing was my husband's hand in my hand and the pain.

"It will still be a while," a voice said. "She's only had one big push."

I heard these words like a bird hears gunshot and had one conscious thought: Oh the fuck it will! I pushed again and entered a pain that was a boundless deep, without form, without I, without separation or control. I didn't think about what I was doing. I was gone and completely present. I was pain. Wild. Immersed so deeply in the moment that there was no singular moment and no singular me. I multiplied as one body separated from my body, and time doubled as the baby started the time that would be called his life. I howled a sound that only comes when you surrender your life to another life.

I held my newborn son. I touched the moss of his hair and felt the fuzz on his big ears. He was so beautiful. He was such a stranger.

And I wasn't afraid.

I was awake.

For a brief moment, I was aware of another human in a way that I had never felt before and have never felt since.

When he was still very small, just four months old, my son woke up at three in the morning, crying and squirming as if something were hurting him from the inside. I held him to soothe him, but it didn't work until, for some reason, it did. He stopped crying but wouldn't sleep.

I put my ear to his belly and listened to small gurgles as if I knew what they meant. I walked a circuit from living room to kitchen, passing the clock on the stove that read 3:15 then 3:58 then 4:10 then 5:02.

I looked at the clock; he looked at the clock. I carried him through the dark rooms, and he looked at everything, awake to the mobile of paper cranes and the immense orange elephant painted on the wall above his crib. He pointed to the animals of our house and repeated a word in a language of his own. I felt I understood. All the animals that night stood up and came alive for him. They were there for him. He found relief in their images.

He grabbed my neck at last and went to sleep. He was comfortable, but I couldn't rest. I laid him down between my husband and me. I watched him breathe. His chest rose and fell as it should, but I still imagined terrible valves at the entrance and exit of his stomach flapping open at the wrong time inside his fourteen-pound, pale body.

Silent lightning illuminated his skin and the bit of black hair on his mostly bald head. He really did look like Wallace Shawn. I held his hand in my hand, letting the comfort of his relaxed hand fill my own. I forced my eyes closed, but under the charged light of sleeplessness, I saw him. He was a newborn again. His face was yellow with jaundice, just like it had been in the few days after his birth. The whites of his eyes were yellow with bilirubin like a dandelion in bloom. The doctors promised he would be fine as long as he ate and peed the toxins out. And if he didn't?

My eyes flared open. In making my child's life, I had made his death. *I could think of little else.* [Hunt]

———————

His forehead is spotted with bruises. Yesterday, the white laundry basket popped him in the mouth. Today, when the basket tilts he lets go, and for a second, he stands on his own. He holds his arms in the air as if saying, *look at me!* Then his leg trembles. Knees buckle. His head hits the doorframe with a sound that strikes me like a two-by-four.

I jump. I force myself to wait. Let him respond before I respond. Let him have his experience without mine. The ache of it. I'm not breathing.

He spreads his hands on the floor. He looks up at me as if the world is breaking up with him.

"Okay?" I ask.

He rubs his eyes.

He sits up and sees the white laundry basket, resting on its side. He crawls to it and stands again. To do it again. He's going to do it again. In the afternoon light, I watch my son begin to fall. I press my hands together so hard that they bleach white in prayer. My thumb finds my pulse, softly chanting:

Fear is a vein in the body of love.

Fear is a vein in the body of love.

I find Mary across the room. She holds her son in her arms. The fingers of her left hand are bent. For a long time, I couldn't tell if they were closing to pull her son closer or opening to let him go. Now I realize it's both.

You must hold him *while* letting him go.

But how? I'm trying to understand.

I'm with Bartholomew, who long ago begged you to speak: *Tell us how you conceived the incomprehensible, or how you carried him who cannot be carried.* [*Bartholomew*]

You warned him: *Ask me not concerning this mystery. If I should begin to tell you, fire will issue forth out of my mouth and consume all the world.* [*Mary*] What you know would destroy everything we have known; it would burn, as mother-knowledge does.

He pressed you to speak until you stood and told him that an angel visited you and was the first to call you the chosen vessel and "grace inexhaustible." The flames must have escaped from your hot mouth then, for your son appeared and put his hand over your face and told you to be quiet.

But I need you to speak.

Burn us up, Mary.

Mother of us, where is your relief? [*Hopkins*]

GUN

I needed something to be beautiful again, so I took my son to *The Nutcracker*, to see the sugar plum children dance.

When he couldn't see past the big head in the next row, I pulled my two-year-old onto my lap. He leaned against my chest, sleepy with the afternoon, that time of day when he usually naps and drifts safely away from this world.

He pointed as a woman in the orchestra lifted two cymbals and quietly put them down. For a brief moment, I only felt the weight of his warm body. I felt his legs dangling against my legs, his knees over my knees. Our bodies moved together. He was a little planet in my orbit, and I was a planet in his. He leaned forward, and I leaned with him, hoping only to inhabit the calm anticipation that comes before something good begins.

The flickering lights stilled the audience. He looked up. I looked around.

I was already tightening my arms around his body, my hands grabbing the flannel of his shirt. I was already imagining where we would hide as the room darkened that December of 2012, just one day after Newtown, the children's elementary school still a crime scene.

The music erupted. The ballet began. A dancer rested all of her weight on the point of her toe. A group of children gathered at the side of the stage and began to hum a song I couldn't hear because I was counting them.

———————

When the radio announcer said "twenty children," I couldn't listen to the rest. Or I wouldn't. I had fully registered the tone of his voice, the way it deflated, ready to stop, to be silent and never speak again.

I turned down the radio as I drove my son to preschool where ten children hang their coats next to his in the morning and are still there in the afternoon when I pick him up.

He doesn't usually go to school on Friday, but this was December. There were extra parties. So much to celebrate. He was invited to lunch where they had cupcakes for the boy who was turning three. Dropping my son off at school meant I could go to lunch too, with my husband. A date. Something lovely. We would eat soup and watch people walk down Main Street and say hello to each other.

I had not yet ordered the terrible egg salad sandwich with a tomato relish that was too sweet when my husband asked, "Did you hear?" We said what little we knew and it revealed nothing. I shoved the news into a well inside of me that was numb and cold.

I kept it there until evening, when my son began to stack his blocks. He built the same tall structure he always builds, his hands moving, able to move, so alive that I had to turn away. I turned away so I wouldn't think of dead children while looking at my living child.

———————

Inside the movie theater, my mom and I waited to watch the latest version of *Les Miserables*. We arrived early to get good seats and got stuck with advertisements for television shows and movies we had no desire to see. In preview after preview someone fired a gun. Even the comedy about identity theft included a woman with lovely breasts who pointed her gun down at the camera and pulled the trigger without blinking. I considered holding up my thumb to block out her gun. I would make it look like the beautiful woman was holding my thumb. But I didn't want to upset the stranger behind me.

I glanced down the row of faces. They almost looked beautiful in their attention, illuminated by movie light. Two seats down, a woman stared at the screen without blinking, her expression so confident; the guns weren't real.

I turned back to the screen only to feel the small tick of nerves behind my ears. I felt a vibration and suddenly believed that someone nearby was getting ready to stand up and do something. I would hide. I would be quiet and lucky. I would find something heavy, maybe a loose theater seat that I would lift with my magical, adrenaline-filled body and slam down on the gunman. Or maybe all I needed was a sharp screw. I would hide beneath the seats and quietly unscrew a piece of metal three inches long. The gunman would back toward me, unaware of my weapon—unaware that I would want him dead. I would wish for a gun, for the distance it can give, as I stabbed his jugular with my screw.

The moment in my mind progressed with a simplicity that fills me with shame. I can't fathom the actual destruction. I imagine surviving. I save and am saved.

A week later, a bell rang over the radio, twenty-six times for twenty children and six adults. Twenty-eight people had died that day, but the mourning count wouldn't include the shooter or his mother.

If the mother was mentioned at all that week, it was to say that she kept an arsenal in her home; she took her friendless son to a shooting range. These facts congealed around her until the question "What kind of person would . . . ?" became the question "What kind of mother . . . ?"

The father was only mentioned to clarify that the boy didn't live with him. This fact of absence was enough to absolve him. It was the mother who couldn't save her son who wouldn't be saved through memory. Her life and her choices were the preface to a massacre. She wouldn't be mourned. She would be subtracted. Even her body was removed from the morgue in the middle of the night and taken to a secret burial site.

In the moment of silence that followed the bell's toll, one mother and one son became one unit of destruction, and the horror was no less.

——————

December was finally over. On New Year's Day, my son woke up early. It was dark and everyone else was still asleep in the seaside vacation cabin, with its slanting kitchen floor and view of the Pacific. The sky was just clear enough to reveal the moon as it set over the black ocean. I pointed to it through the window, holding my child who held me. We sat together in the dark, looking out at the moon in the sky and the moon in the ocean.

"The moon's setting," I said. "Soon, we won't see it at all." I held my hand between his face and the moon. "Goodbye," I said and blocked it from view. A shadow fell over his face. "Hello," I said. I took my hand down and the light returned.

"Do it again," he said, and I continued to show him that when something is in orbit it can be eclipsed, seem gone. Seem as one.

He started to get down from the couch. I wasn't ready to stop holding him.

"Have you heard the story about the moon?" I asked. He shook his head.

"One evening the moon looked down on Auntie Jill's chickens. He noticed a huge egg in the field. It was so round that the moon thought, 'That egg looks like me.' And then he thought,

'Wait! I look like an egg!' Just then, a chicken sat on the egg. 'Oh,' he thought. 'If I'm an egg, then my mother must be a chicken! I want to find her!'

"So the moon looked around the world for his chicken-mother. He looked in the ocean and on mountaintops. He looked in little-boy hair and between little-boy toes. But he couldn't find his chicken mother.

"After a long time, he decided he'd never find her. He began to cry.

"It took a while for him to open his eyes and see the earth still glowing below. Each day, he watched her glow, and each night he grew and grew. When he was a full moon, he saw the grasses stand taller. The waves crested higher to reach him, and every animal looked to the sky until the whole of the earth looked up at the moon. He threw open his wings of light and wrapped them around the earth, holding her in a hug that she returned. Forever."

I hugged my son who hugged me back.

He leaned away from me and looked at the moon. Its light poured onto his face.

For a moment, I believed in the story of its company—the way all are held in its light—even those who are held by no one else.

I wasn't exactly thinking of gunmen as we entered the Drift-wood Public Library in Lincoln City, Oregon. I was looking at the aluminum thermal shields on the windows of the rusting Cadillac parked next to us. Actually, it was two spaces down. I intentionally left a spot between us when I noticed the car was running and going nowhere. I was alone with my son. I kept an eye over my shoulder as I unbuckled his car seat and released his arm from the strap.

A woman got out of the car and walked toward the grocery store. Her eyes were on her feet. She wore an oversized coat of wool. She tucked her nose into its collar.

I came so close to thinking about her warmth on that cold day. But she walked on and we went into the library, with its children's section filled with sunlight and toys, a stuffed crab and platypus, blocks and a small kitchen.

After a while, a girl came in with her sister. They were alone. The older girl asked if my son would like to play.

"No," he said, shyly.

"I'm six," the older one said. "I'm in kindergarten." She spoke with the confidence of a reality TV star. "I don't get along with my teacher," she said.

"Huh," I said. "Why's that?"

She kicked her body toward me and tilted her small head. "I don't give no thought to that," she said and lowered her gaze at me, her eyes vibrating the way a firecracker does once the fuse is lit. I read the warning, but the way she spoke was too familiar to ignore.

"What do you mean?" I asked. Her hands slapped her hips as her body turned to me, coming closer. Her eyelids pinched toward the pupils.

"Don't go asking me questions," she warned. "I don't like anyone asking me questions." She turned to the blocks. They clicked in her hand as she stacked them.

"Sometimes I like questions," I said, pulling out my phone to seem careless even as I felt a weird need to teach her to calm down. I liked her. I wanted to give her a hug.

"What are you building?" I asked, without mentioning that this was a question.

"A rocket ship."

My son came over from the play kitchen. I put my phone back in my pocket. I sat up straight and edged closer to the table where she worked. She showed him where to put a block. I placed my hand on his back. He put it where she said.

"Will it go to the moon?" I asked.

"No," she said. "It's going to the ocean."

"Like a submarine?" She leaned forward without blinking. She had the kills in her eyes. "I mean a rocket-submarine," I corrected, "launching from seafloor to space in one minute." Her sister smiled and the girl's eyes softened a bit. She picked up a pink block and looked away. She thought of names for the ship, first mentioning all the ones she wouldn't use because they belonged to horrible cousins or awful aunts, and while she was volatile, it was painfully clear that she wanted to be cordial, even friendly. She wanted so much to be liked.

She didn't mind when my son took a block or two. He leaned forward until their bodies were inches apart. At times their fingers touched as he placed a block on her rocket-submarine. As she finished the tall structure, he reached up, ready to knock the whole thing down.

"No," I flinched. "Let her build. Please don't knock it down." He sat back and waited.

"Time for lift off!" she said. She balanced the improbable structure between her hands and landed it on the floor. My son inched forward on his knees, reaching, carelessly for what she had made.

I watched my mind turn her kind hand into a quick fist. I'd never be able to get between her and my son fast enough.

"No!" I said, even though nothing had happened. Nothing had changed. The girl and my son looked at me, confused, straining to understand. "Almost time to go," I said. "Almost time for lunch. We need to go soon." He reached again for her blocks. "Please don't," I said. He paused and looked at me.

"He might knock it down. He's still a little boy," I said to the little girl.

I waited for her eyes to look at him as they had looked at me, and I was ready. He was already too close to this girl, but that wasn't right, and I knew it. He was too close to my idea of her—that she would harm anyone who got too close to her, that she wanted to harm someone because she too is filled with the kind of anger that still burns from an early loss or terror, experienced as a child, when life takes something away that will never be returned: a parent, dignity, safety, or even a belief, not only gone but destroyed. A part of you dies even though you live, and the destruction moves all too easily from one person to another. I'm not comfortable thinking this way, but there it is: the idea that the wounded will wound.

I prepared to leave and get away from my response to the girl in the library, even as she calmly watched my son knock over her blocks and helped him put them away. Even as she was so comforted by his presence, I was grabbing his coat.

"Let's say goodbye," I said. "Time to go."

She went to the play kitchen, and before he could follow, I tried to pick him up and hold him.

"Time to go," I repeated as he wrenched free and ran, his small legs speeding around a bookshelf and turning back to the kitchen and the girl. He was on his knees with another toy in his hands when I reached down to pick him up.

"Stay," he said. "No," he cried.

"We need to go home and have lunch," I told him.

"No," he said.

"It's alright. Thanks for letting us play," I said to the girl who held up her hand in a brief wave. She smiled sadly, and even as I knew I was the cause, I turned away, cinching my son to my body and exiting the library, rushing past the parked car with its sun shields now taken down and the windows opened for some fresh air, and into our car where I strapped my son into his seat, locked the doors, and returned to the cabin on a cliff, overlooking the Pacific so gentle and wide.

It wasn't time for lunch at all. We sat on the front lawn. My son played alone, and I looked out at the ocean, trying to forget the world only to have it well back up inside. The girl was with me even though I refused to be with her.

In my mind, I always survive. I escape. I get away. And I do no good.

I watch the ocean waves repeat their calm as if the calm is inside.

CENTAUR

To be wild takes thistle and sand, not this hay and fence. This horse and I are domesticated. We are animals who know the rules: I will brush her and she will be brushed. I will remove that blanket and get the dust off her flanks, and I will tell myself that their constant twitching in sunlight or wind is just a reflex and not preparation, not a rising in her of all the fears in me—of all the ways that we will hurt each other.

I feel the horse feeling my fear as I stand outside of her gate. Crows gather on a nearby branch. They talk in low tones, the way an audience does before a show. I shake with nerves.

I should be fine. This horse belongs to a little girl. She rides her every day, sometimes without a saddle. The girl holds the horse's mane in her hands and cinches her legs around a body that lets her float over fields. They go together, without pull or force.

Besides, my friend promised that this horse would be easy to care for while his family was away. "To care for," he said. But I heard him say she would be easy to take care of. I would put her hay in the stall as he showed me and break the thin layer of ice in the bucket so she can drink, so she can pull water through teeth that break entire apples in half.

Wilder horses use their teeth as a weapon. I once watched a documentary about an experienced trainer who knew that to handle a horse requires a tender firmness called "give." He was calm and steady, even when the horse rose up on her hind legs, opened her mouth, and plunged her front teeth into his forehead. The skin flapped back, revealing the bone of his skull.

"There's one thing to watch out for," my friend said. The horse chewed the air, strengthening her vise-grip jaw.

"What's that?" I asked.

"She casts," my friend walked around the barn and through the gate.

"Right," I said, as if I understood.

He latched the gate, locking us all inside. "It's when a horse rolls onto her back and gets stuck."

"And that's bad," I said.

"Too long like that . . . she'll die." He held one hand over the other and smacked. "Her organs would crush her heart."

We walked closer to her. She snapped her head up and down as if seeing something. Her brown eyes reflected a cloud, or maybe that was a warning. I couldn't tell. I don't know horses. All I know of them I learned from the Rolling Stones and Anne of Green Gables. "Wild horses couldn't drag me away," sing the Stones. "Wild horses won't drag the secret from me," Anne says. "How would wild horses drag a secret from a person anyhow?"

"What do I do?" I asked.

He pointed to a yellow rope hanging from the barn wall. "Use that. Tie it around a leg and then roll her toward you until she stands."

I nodded, imagining her hooves swinging through the air.

"Don't worry," he said.

Now the horse's family is gone on their vacation. The horse and I are alone. I'm shivering, and not because it's cold out. I have to take off her green blanket and brush her body. I have to reach under her wide chest to unsnap the straps that hold her blanket in place. I have to touch her.

I begin to lift the thin rope that holds the gate closed. She stomps. She pounds the ground flat and shows what hooves can do. I step inside and close the gate. The crows clap their wings. The horse exhales a fog.

I hold up the brush. "Time to brush you," I say. I sound calm. I can sound calm.

She twitches. She lifts and lowers her head. "I have this brush," I say. The brush leaves its mark on my tightening hand. "Just a brush," I say. My voice doesn't sound like my voice. I take a slow step and she begins to trot. Or is that a canter? She comes at me. The branches crackle beneath her like a pulse. "Stop," I say. "I don't have carrots." I step back, slamming into a fencepost. She comes at me and there's no way to stop what's happening even as I see it will happen.

The brush hits the ground. I raise my emptied hands. Her face comes at my face. Lashes on her eyelids. Nostrils. Delicate hairs on her nose. She lowers her head and rams it into my chest, hitting the bone of her long face into the long bone of my sternum. She pins me to the fencepost. I can feel the heat of her body through my coat. She presses harder, and I gasp as my spine pushes against the rough wood of the fence, so different from the smooth logs that make the home nearby.

I sat in that house, just moments ago, and watched hummingbirds drink red sugar-water. I sat beneath a down blanket, feeling the warmth of little birds even though they are dead. I listened for the coyotes to yelp their human cries. It was only the distance between us that let me find comfort in the connection.

Now, I'm not sure where the horse's body stops and mine begins. Her head plunges into my chest. Her mouth enters my heart with a message: I know you, girl—you closed up clam. You can't get away. Stop hiding.

Horse lovers say: A horse will show you who you are.

Her head digs deep. I can't feel my face. Or think. Let me think.

Even snails speak.

Bears mourn the dead.

Some male birds try to mate with each other, and they aren't concerned with making anything other than contact.

I'm about to be crushed. I'm going to be destroyed by what I must care for.

I feel the give and give way. I fold over her. I lean into her head with my chest. I drape my head over her neck. My hands find her ears. I idle my thumbs in their warmth.

Our bodies slow down. Our breath follows the same clock. The first snow falls on our common body and into the field of bunchgrass where we stand.

"Show me," I whisper into her neck. My thumbs trace the widening edges of her ears, down to her mane. I tuck each thumb into that coarse hair and thread my fingers behind, slowly tightening the clamp of each hand. I take a single breath. I am the girl who feels the softness of ears, and I am the girl who grabs hold of her mane and pulls her away hard. She steps back. She lets me go.

OZZY OSBOURNE

He bit the head off a bat.

He bit the head off a dove.

Unlike the dove, a bat has teeth. A nose. A bat has long wings that spread to reveal tender bones like those of the human hand. It has eyelids. And hair. A bat has a face. A face like a human's went into the dark of a human face. A mouth into a mouth. A voice into a voice.

And did I tell Joy about it or did Jimmy tell us? We church-bound kids of the 1980s knew nothing of Ozzy Osbourne, "Prince of Darkness," former lead singer of a band called Black Sabbath, until the televangelist leaned into the microphone and whispered "DEVIL." After that, we learned all we could. We gathered under the secretive lights of the carport. We leaned into each other's faces and whispered Ozzy. The name fizzed in our mouths, sweet and possibly rotting.

Ozzy bit the head off a bat. He bit the head off a dove.

The dove happened before the bat. Ozzy had stashed three doves in his pocket and carried them into the offices of his new record label. He would be more than their devil. He would surprise them with this symbol of peace and light. The doves waited in his pocket, three apples in the dark. Two flew up as planned, flapping around the room as if looking for an exit. Ozzy held onto the third.

It was a big day. A photographer was present, and how exciting it must have been when the rock star, already so photogenic in his white plaid dinner jacket and jeans and long brown hair softly framing his face, looked to the third dove. In the first of four photos, Ozzy cups the bird in both hands with a tenderness usually reserved for the wounded. In the second photo, the bird head is in his mouth. The woman sitting next to Ozzy is still leaning toward him in the third photo and still smiling even though she is looking directly at the bird's severed head as it falls from Ozzy's mouth, photographed in midair, hovering next to a cross that hangs from a chain around Ozzy's neck. It's only in the last photo that the woman silently registers the kill. Maybe four seconds have passed. Ozzy's eyes cross and leave nothing straight.

"Evil," said the televangelist. "Ozzy is the devil."

The first time he said devil, the word was a hammock beneath my brain. It carried the weight of a darkness I didn't know how to lift. For a moment, I rested. Hung out. Got lazy. The word devil let me contain without consideration all the *dualities we can conceive but not perceive. [Barthes]*

But when the preacher repeated *Devil*, the word swiped over my body, leaving its trace like the hands of older girls who sometimes pushed me when I walked by in the school hallway. They never said a word. They hit and kept walking as if nothing had changed. But my body registered the message: "Nothing," their touch said. "You mean nothing."

"Devil," said the preacher until he turned red. The only devil that came to mind was the cartoon red guy with a pitchfork and no pants. Devil of movies and games. Devil of play. Devil. Devil. Repeated, the word no longer felt like a word.

The same thing happened when I practiced my signature. I wrote my name over and over until the words weren't words. My brain got tired and no longer attached the word to any known meaning.

I didn't know the term for this experience. I didn't have the words: semantic exhaustion. Or semantic satiation. Or bleaching, depletion, a glare. I didn't yet know how to say *Jamais vu*, meaning *never-seen*. But I know the feeling. *Jamais vu*. This is what it feels like to categorize someone. To erase them.

"Devil," said the preacher.

"Ozzy," we said.

The moths banged their heads against the carport lights. A mile away, the town I came from was sinking into the emptiness of strip malls and church signs whose warnings shamed us.

We had a different story to tell.

Ozzy bit the head off a bat.

A fan threw the bat onto the stage. Dazed by the spotlight, the bat didn't move. Ozzy picked it up and thought it was rubber until he put the head of the bat into his mouth and the bat bit back. For months, Ozzy had to get painful rabies shots in his stomach.

To draw out the moment of pain for each other, we imagined a needle the width of an old oak tree jabbed into his gut. Maybe we loved to repeat this story because we felt like the bat, shoved into a darkness it couldn't understand. Or maybe we thought we loved animals and wanted to protect them. Maybe we still believed that all creatures are equal and deserve to be loved. Maybe we were learning to say that there is great suffering all around.

Ozzy snorted a line of ants like cocaine, and every day he drank four gallons of whiskey and topped it off with morphine and sleeping pills and rohypnol. Ozzy baptized audiences with pig intestines and crawled under his piano in a white suit with a shotgun in one hand and a knife in the other to kill seventeen of his own cats. Ozzy ran into his wife's room, wearing only his underwear. "They say I must kill you," he told her. He doesn't remember trying to strangle her. He doesn't remember that she bashed a bottle over his head. He only remembers the glaring voices, telling him what to do. The voices confirmed that the devil was inside of him. "The devil is in all of us," he said. "All of the time. Us," he said. "Us."

Yes. We said. Us. The devil is inside. We'd heard it before.

We knew the other Prince of Darkness and his burning lake. God used to call him the brightest angel, morning star, opening act for the sun. Lucifer. As if naming him "Light!" weren't enough, God covered Lucifer in gemstones of diamonds and sapphires; his foot made of brass rested on God's head. He was as bright as any being then. But under the light we were taught to read as infinite knowledge there could be no questions. Only certainty. Only faith. When Lucifer refused to accept what he was told, God threw him out. Lucifer fell out of heaven and toward our earth, screaming his confusion and loneliness into us.

But we didn't want allegory. We needed a new song. We needed a way to converse with our refusals. We weren't children anymore. We were preteens. We measured the height of our bangs with a straight ruler and no longer wore our pants with pleats. We carried black eyeliner in our bags and were about to put it on.

This was the year before we got cable. Before we found MTV. Before we heard Ozzy scream at a pitch that reverbs. Verbs. Comes alive and will not be caught.

At the edge of the carport, bats swung by the eaves, opening their mouths to make sounds too high in pitch for any human to hear. We heard only their wings, like dry hands rubbing against someone's cheek.

"Ozzy," we whispered, opening our dark mouths. "A head went inside a head." And when we said that "a mouth went into a mouth," something started to break down inside. It was a kind of order. The story of the bat unwound all we were taught to believe and could no longer accept as our own. The story stabbed the inner ear where equilibrium lives until we were as disoriented as we knew ourselves to be.

In that vibrating moment, the whole of human suffering seemed as if it might come clean out of our mouths to be heard even as it receded deeper inside and decibel-loved the bones with a sound that might speak for the ache.

DICK,
ABOUT YOUR HEART,

1.

Too much plaque between your teeth can cause plaque buildup in your heart, so we clean our mouths, hoping to open the heart's four chambers. Four chambers in your heart and four chambers in mine, and we make eight. We stand in similar, tile-laden rooms that echo equally the sounds of water and the sounds we make. We open our mouths to tend to the hidden spaces within. This is the most tender thing we do for ourselves all day. We're not in a hurry. We don't need cups, just the hollow of a hand, the same one we used when we were children—the same one I will use to teach my son how to hold water in the cup of his hand and to hold a flower gently enough not to kill it. Together, we pretend that this state of tenderness is enough to keep us well.

2.

On the radio, you announce that you're thinking of getting a heart transplant. You're no longer vice president, but you still strain syllables through the clenched teeth that said "War on Terror," "Enhanced Interrogation," "No regrets."

The bass of your voice rattles the speakers and throws gravel into my bathroom, pinging the walls. Sound doesn't have to be understood to reverberate. It bounces off the tile walls to form standing waves and echoes, much like it did in the sonic chapels of the 17th century, the opera houses and concert halls, the kinds of chambers shaped to create internal reflections.

Perhaps this is why the ventricles of our hearts are also called chambers. And why the word chamber was once the name for the bedroom where bodies rest and are made and sometimes die.

All too soon, chamber came to mean the domain of the monarch, and from there it didn't take long for it to also indicate the part of the gun that holds the charge and the many rooms where regulations are made.

But, Dick Cheney, the word chamber also describes an opera written for a small number of singers. And for orchestras with only a few musicians. A chamber is where arguments are heard as well as music. An intimate venue, it's the hollow near the ear canal, which, in a completely silent room, captures the sound of the heart beating through the body, beating at the same tempo as the song "Staying Alive." This is the same song instructors use to teach students the rate at which to pump the chest of an unconscious person.

3.

For someone who never wrote things down, never used e-mail, wouldn't willingly talk to the press, kept the names of your staff out of federal directories, and stored your papers in a locked safe, you're talking an awful lot about your heart these days. At fourteen you watched your great-grandfather die of a heart attack. At thirty-seven you had your first. You went on to have four more. A quadruple bypass. An episode of ventricular fibrillation, a condition in which the heart moves wormlike.

V-fib is not a failure of the heart muscle. It's a failure of the heart's signals to coordinate. The heart can't pump. The lower chambers lose the ability to contract in the unison needed to force blood into the kidneys and brain and every major organ. Within three seconds, a person blacks out. Is without a pulse. Is on the floor, turning blue. The heart that can't communicate leaves a body on the ground.

You say you might get a new heart. "The technology is better now," you say, "good enough to take the risk," even at your age. But the truth is, you're almost too old to be on the donor list at all, and although you *need* a new heart, you won't say "need." You say "maybe." "Maybe I'll get a heart transplant," as if the choice between life and death is always yours to make.

You say you feel great. Normal. You describe your life. You go to the grocery store and make chili, or spaghetti sauce, at home in Wyoming, where the elk come to your back door and don't realize you're a hunter.

You have survived: five heart attacks, two angioplasties, a pacemaker . . .

You might have another heart attack any second.

Like right now.

Or now.

Your heart won't beat at full strength ever again, and you're alive only because you have a battery-powered heart pump with twelve-volt batteries and a minicomputer that pumps blood through your body so continuously that it leaves you without a pulse. You have no pulse. You take a drug called warfarin that I pronounce "war-faring." The pump and the warfarin keep you alive. "I have batteries that power on a regular basis," you say. When you take the battery out, the pump begins to beep. You laugh. "It's alright," you say. "It's not going to blow up."

It's too easy to laugh. Even the broadcasters take a swing when they ask, "Dick Cheney's Heart: Is It Working?" How easy it is to editorialize your public heart when nothing meaningful is being said.

But let's get this out of the way. Your broken heart is a metaphor and reality. I am interested in symbols. And I am interested in the actuality of your heart.

4.

When a teacher asked our class to think of someone problematic, I thought of you. "Find a picture of this person," she said. "See this person, physically and without judgment." She promised that if I looked at you this way for a very long time, you would become radiant.

It's late at night when I find the picture of you online that I think I can stare at this way. It isn't an official photo from the Office of the Vice President, or the one of you with photoshopped fangs or the one where you look like Darth Vader or the one where you're wearing a leather vest and holding your hands above your head, looking ready for sex. I pick a picture of you in a white cowboy hat. I like cowboy hats and the wide-open spaces they fill. I like that you seem relaxed in the picture, maybe even receptive.

I make a blind contour drawing of you. I place the pencil on the page and don't look at it. For five minutes, I look only at you. I start by drawing the brim of your white hat and then the curve of your jaw. I move the pencil as if pressing it against the contours of your face, as if touching your face. For five minutes, I feel exposed to a form of radiation. It hits at such a low frequency that it can't be known until it aggregates.

When I'm done, I see that I've drawn your nose and mouth in the right place, but one eyeball has dropped onto your cheek and another onto your nose. They cut into your skin like bad body piercings. A few eyelashes streak away from the eye sockets that are in the right place and empty.

In the lines, I see the way my hand moves a pencil to draw the shape of your face. I see how my body perceives your body. A living morphology seems at work in this drawing. Not metamorphosis, which happens so intently on its own, but a patient way of looking that might transform the seen right along with the seer. Goethe, who first defined morphology, wrote, *The eyes of the spirit have to work in perpetual living connexion [sic] with those of the body, for one otherwise risks seeing past a thing.*

Have you read Goethe? If I could send you anything, I would send you the pages he writes on morphology. He asks us to be honest: we can only *portray rather than explain*. [*Goethe*]

In my portrayal, your mouth is a single line. Thin. As if without teeth. Clamped shut. Jaw set and certain.

My mouth makes the same tight shape when I walk around this Midwestern town I call home. I live here with my husband and son. My baby doesn't sleep much, so I don't either. I go for late walks with him strapped to my chest so the sound of my heart fills his ear. Even as I have this thought, I'm drawn to the apartment lights, unable to believe they will last. The buildings go dark in my mind. The whole city loses power. Loses heat. Every time I walk, I can only seem to imagine devastation as if there isn't already so much darkness in the world.

Or is there just too little light in me?

I look at the drawing I have made of your face, Dick Cheney, and only think with gleeful precision that the four chambers of your heart refuse to function as they should.

How difficult it is not to darken the world with our words.

5.

In the government study that details the impacts of your policies, long, black boxes redact much of the text. Drawn with Sharpie precision, I find them to be the most honest marks on the page; they embody a silence that screams of decision. The black boxes are followed by descriptions of detainees who were kept shackled in complete darkness in cells made of plywood painted black and called "Black Boxes." It was winter. There was no heat. There was the sound of loud music, played constantly, at a volume known to disrupt the human heartbeat. The musical torture included pop songs like Christina Aguilera's "Dirrty," and the classic "We Are the Champions," twenty-four hours a day.

Very rarely, between the songs magnified into torture, the men could hear the call to prayer. Dawn. Noon. Afternoon. Sunset. Night. The prayer marked time for them, and they could hear its marking as circulatory, continuing. Time had not stopped. They were not yet dead. They heard the *Adhān*, a prayer whose name extends from a word that means *ear, listen, hear, be informed.*

Listen, when you read the redacted words no one else can see, how do they inform you? At what point does the heart register the cold? What else do you know about the man who froze to death in his detention cell? His name is not redacted. Find it there. Speak it. Hear it. Do you know where he was buried? Do you know the names of his four daughters? His wife? When was the last time you spoke to your wife? How would you describe her voice? The voices of your daughters? The sound of anyone you love? The sound of love? What does it sound like to be American? What does it sound like to be Terrorist? In a concrete cell in Afghanistan, north of Kabul, the night of November 19, when the temperature was 36 degrees, why was this man left naked, shackled to the wall in a way that forced the lower half of his body onto the bare concrete at a temperature that makes the body lose heat faster than it can produce it?

At this point, a person begins to shiver, feel hungry, has trouble speaking. The heart rate increases. Then the shivering stops. The pulse gets weak.

There are so many descriptions of the dark, but there is only one way out. The only escape is presented as an answer, isn't it? Just give me an answer. Tell us what you know. And we'll let you go.

I don't want answers. I want description. I want the arc of the human, resonating somewhere in the back of your body. I want to hear your visceral, human response.

Tell me. Where do you feel something? A small change in pressure? A small force of blood? I want to hear a statement from your soul.

6.

I left America for a few weeks because I thought I could. As the sun set on the pastel buildings of Cape Town's Bo-Kaap neighborhood, the *Adhān* began to filter through a loud speaker. Beyond the windows, inside each home, people touched their foreheads to sacred rugs. No one was in the street. I was alone when I heard the call, which I had never heard before, and so I heard it through the amplification of an America that equates Islam with terror. As the voice spiked to reach a note different from any I had ever heard, I was ashamed and angry at the way fear crawled like ants inside my ears and would not let me hear this call as a prayer and not a threat. I wasn't kneeling. I was a woman. Alone. My hair was showing. American. I tried to find my ear. I tried to listen through my fear.

I closed my eyes and remembered my red, two-door coupe. It could take me far away from everything, every thought, and into the density of a night that might destroy me and, at the very same time, let me hear the good sounds coming from the tape deck. Radiohead. Nirvana. 1995.

I sang along. I listened. I heard my own emotions sung back to me: I suffered but I knew little of fear.

I still know nothing of actual terror. I know nothing of fight. Imagination is the sidearm I carry.

7.

The whole house is asleep. I'm the only one awake. I find comfort in the asparagus fern draped over the mantel of the fireplace that no longer works and will never burn again. I find comfort in all the plants and the pots that hold them. I find comfort in the fan that runs a hum through the summer night; my son, sleeping; knowing that you are sleeping. And I'm awake, imagining you. You stand on a stage. You, my blind contour drawing . . . You are about to sing.

You stand in the dark of a theater, unable to see the crowd looking up at you even though you can feel them like a dark sea prepared to swallow you whole. You're shaking. You lower your white hat and wrap your hand around your wrist, squeezing for the pulse that isn't there. You don't seem to come from a family of singers. Your father was a soil conversation agent and mother a 1930s softball star.

You are, it seems, as I am when I stand on a stage and am asked to sing even though I come from a family of singers. I was raised in the choir. For a long time, I sang solos. But somehow my love of singing turned into a fear of it. When I try to sing, I hear the blood in my throat. Feel dizzy. My heart strains against the walls of my chest as if trying to get out. I'm having a heart attack, I think. My heart is a bomb, I think.

For a long time, I thought I was afraid of making a mistake; I might forget the words or miss a note. But again and again, what happens to me when I sing is much worse. I start to cry. It's embarrassing. I sing a note and the sound of it merges with the feeling of it in my throat and the back of my neck, straight down into my chest where it breaks my heart as if my heart has never been broken. Every hurt binds to every joy. The amplified emotion forms a wavelength and travels. It can't be obscured or silenced. It's physical. The sound changes the air pressure. It vibrates down to the bones. My bones and your bones. It's felt in the teeth. This vulnerable melody frightens me. And it's this vulnerable melody that I will make you sing, deep in my mind, tonight. To make you this vulnerable, to imagine you afraid, is the only way I can stop being afraid of you.

You are going to sing a song that I have always sung when no one else is around. It's a traditional American folksong of suffering. It has been sung for generations, its composer unknown. It has over 160 different lyrics, but in every version, someone dies and a girl goes missing. In every version, longing turns into a demand.

You are going to sing this song. But imagination is a funny thing, Dick. To imagine you up there, I have to imagine myself standing up there. I have to stand under the same spotlight, preparing to sing. Already, I feel my pulse banging in my wrists. A spoon hits a glass. Someone coughs. My hands and face go cold. My heart loses the regular beat that lets me forget it exists. I step to the microphone. I must find the long note. If only I can hold it, something more than fear will resonate. I must sing. For you to sing, I must sing:

My girl, my girl, don't lie to me
Tell me where did you sleep last night

In the pines, in the pines
Where the sun don't ever shine
I would shiver the whole night through

My girl, my girl, where will you go
I'm going where the cold wind blows

In the pines, in the pines
Where the sun don't ever shine
And the birds sleep the whole day through

8.

The next morning, I wake up feeling cold and blank. I move in a fog through the entire day until the day is gone. It's dark when I start to feel alive again.

I make pasta for dinner. I fill the steel pot with cold water. I put it over the flame on the stove and wait. I open a beer. Turn on the radio.

"Dick Cheney," the announcer says, "had a heart transplant today."

For one false moment, I think of coincidence, of alignment. But really, it's kismet in the Arabic tradition of the word *qasama*, meaning division. Portion. Lot. Divide. Because while I would like to say that I hear your news and hold my head in my hands to send you healing thoughts, I am only thinking: the wrong person has been healed. Over and over. The wrong person has been healed.

The announcer assures everyone listening that you are "resting at home."

". . . doing fine."

You will "make a full recovery."

The water on the stove boils over. And I let it.

WILD THINGS ARE

TONIGHT, MY SON wears his owl pajamas and makes *mischief of one kind and another.* [*Sendak*] He swings the stuffed pig and oinks; he builds block towers to knock them down. I call him "WILD THING!" I love him so much. "I COULD EAT YOU UP!" I say. He wraps his potato fingers around the laundry basket and stands. "Careful . . . ," I say. *All fear is caused by our loving something.* [*Thomas Aquinas*] The objects of play have teeth. Plastic thorns stick out from that laundry basket's edge. Wooden blocks have smooth letters but trip like roots. The bookshelf stands on hind legs.

But the rug-burn carpet is his ocean.

He is in his boat,   and I am in mine.

We sail along, he over starfish and me over sharks, to an island that's not so far away.

At the first bright cove, he anchors where I can't seem to go. I'm bound for a dark and opposite shore where a thicket of blue ferns is shaded by hatch marks. Terrible teeth and eyes and roars come closer. I tell myself: *BE STILL!* I must stare into their *yellow eyes without blinking.* [*Sendak*] I must protect my son.

BE STILL! I tell myself as chickens clack through the yard. My son toddles between them, his hands clenching their favorite treat of dried worms. He wants to eat their worms but isn't allowed.

"Feed the worms to the chickens," says his uncle. "Like this." He turns up my son's palm. "Good," says his uncle. When my son's hands are empty, he holds them up and says, "A," that letter of beginning—first letter of the first name of the first boy who for a time was curious, not yet afraid of losing what he loved.

More chickens approach with their terrible claws and terrible beaks. They snap the worms from his hands and shake their necks. Just one wrong peck, I think, and I will snap that neck. You, terrible, yellow-eyed bird. I eat the yolks out of your eggs!

"Good," says his uncle. The chickens almost knock my son over. He doesn't mind. He holds out his hand for more.

I pick him up. I point to the chickens and laugh, but I'm not fooling anyone. I'm trying to keep him safe even though there's no real danger.

I hold him. I smell his hair. He's already a boy and not a baby. He no longer smells of milk and clean laundry. He smells of sweat and motion, those pungent smells of distance. He struggles to get down. He runs to the chickens. They surround him. They nip at his empty fingers. He flinches and opens his hands even wider.

A TERRIBLE FOOT BREAKS through the ferns. Flat. Furred. With spines. I try to see the ferns as ferns but I can't tell the difference between fronds and feet. Their long talons reach for my legs. Their spores become terrible yellow eyes.

Have they seen my son? He's barely two feet tall. He's wearing pajamas. He has brown hair. Gray eyes.

I never believed in gray eyes before he was born. I thought they were something novelists gave to characters to make them memorable. Then he opened his gray eyes and moved them across the face of the world. They are cautious but focused, and maybe this is why I call him Beetle. Or maybe it's because of the thinness of his face. Or maybe it's because beetles are from the order called *Coleoptera*, which is Greek for the sheathed wing that is slightly protected in order to soar.

MY DOG HAS DART EYES. He tracks my Beetle with them.

My son raises his hand and sticks his fingers through the slats of the flimsy baby gate that separates them. I know he wants to pet the dog and lean over him like another soft cushion, but the dog licks my son's fingers to taste them not kiss.

"No," I say. The dog stops but doesn't look away, and I can feel what he wants. When he was still a puppy he slept in my arms, but he bit anything that moved. At the vet's office, he growled at the metal examination table and nipped the vet.

"Have you ever owned a blue heeler?" he asked.

"No," I said.

The vet sighed the sigh of those who don't believe you will ever really understand the rules of the world, but they must explain anyway. "You have to be tough," he said. "Decisive. Use force. Like this." He grabbed the scruff of my puppy's neck and flipped him onto his back.

I learned. I was sure. I was calm. I muzzled my dog's mouth with my hand. I felt the muscles flex in his jaw as I firmly said, "No." I trained him to walk beside me and not nip at the thin skin of my ankles. I taught him to play safely. He learned to chase the tennis balls I threw across fields instead of the children running by. I taught him how to stay.

"Stop," I say.

But my dog keeps staring at my son the way he stares at the squirrels he chases down to kill. He did the same thing to a rabbit three days after my son was born.

I step over the gate and send the dog outside. "Enough," I say. "Now stop."

I BLINK AND *RUMPUS!* All the creatures gnash their terrible teeth and blink their terrible eyes.

There are no words here, just images.

AT THE PARK, MY SON SWINGS SLOWLY. My dog is quick. He ignores his leash and lunges to bite the legs dangling down. The dog is sitting again before I realize what has happened. For a moment, it's as if nothing has happened.

But there is a rectangle of cloth missing from my son's corduroy pants. Beneath the tear, the skin is fine. There's no blood this time. No one cries. The dog didn't hurt my son. And I understand for certain that he could.

STOP! I say, and the wild things play.

.

TO GIVE MY DOG AWAY I drive eight hours to the south. I roll down the windows as I did the day I got him, when he bit me with milk teeth all the way home. I rubbed his fat belly as we drove by a river so beautiful that I named him for it. At first, we lived in a tent. I was a farmhand, and he was my puppy. While I weeded, he sat at the edge of the field. He barked when I went too far away. "It's okay," I told him. "I'm right here." His puppy belly warmed mine when we slept. He loved me, and I loved him and thought that love could make him kind.

Now, when I look at him, love comes to mind but that love is for my son.

I see my dog in the rearview, his tongue panting between rows of terrible teeth.

I turn my eyes back to the road.

I SEE THE BRIGHTER SHORE. Through the ferns, my son's boat floats in its cove. And I see him! LOVE! I sing with the sun. How much I want to be joyful with love. This is the shore I come from!

A furry palm grabs hold of my ankle. "Let me rumpus!" I beg. "Goddammit. Let us go!"

"You cannot go!" cry the terrible mouths with their terrible teeth. *"We'll eat you up!"* [*Sendak*]

And I say, "I know."

I NIGHT WALK from the bedroom where I do not sleep to the bedroom where my son doesn't sleep. By the time I get there, he isn't crying anymore. I reach into the crib only to feel the sheet stretched tight over the mattress. I can't find him. He has made his way out of the crib. Or he was taken. There's no way to get to him. I will never find him again. I'm living in the last moment of my life.

I flip on the light. He's there. Sitting in the far corner. He blinks up at me. My gray-eyed beetle. Wild king of this night. You are where someone loves you best of all.

MY SON STEPS *INTO HIS PRIVATE BOAT,* and I step into mine. [*Sendak*] We sail side by side. I keep watch over his happiness. I watch out for the loss of his body, and I watch for the loss of his joy. When one is gone, the other doesn't matter.

I *trick* this *idea into being* so *that the old joy, modest as cake, as wine and friendship, will stay with us at last, backed by the night.* [*Ashbery*]

MY SON HOLDS THE BOOK I LOVE *in and out of weeks and through a day and into the night of* our *very own* living room. [*Sendak*] He turns the pages. He touches the sharp beaks. In this book, all of the terrible things have a plausible shape and narrative. A child defies his mother. He escapes her fears and enters a land of his own where he stares into all of the yellow eyes. He plays at terror. And lives.

[*Alkhatib*]

SAN ANDREAS FAULT

Before we settled into love, we went to the lizards and Joshua trees. So new to each other (four months) and so young, we drove along a hidden fault line. We loved our freedom and were beginning to love each other. We set up a quiet tent for a few days. I wore black underwear and lay on my belly while reading.

I don't remember what I read. I only remember the photograph you took of me through the mesh of the tent. When I looked at myself as you looked at me, I felt beautiful, but I couldn't forget about the tension of the future, snapping between us. We would leave that moment and that place we loved and didn't yet know if we were going together.

Down below, the fault line crushed rock and clay into flour. In time, that pressure would erupt into an earthquake with enough force and magnitude to knock us out of this life like loose baby teeth. But in that moment, it just squeezed water to the surface, making the Oasis of Mara. The palm trees spread their shade and cooled the air by fifteen degrees. We made dinner. Love. Breakfast.

Now we're living through another damp winter. I make breakfast. Snack. Lunch. Snack. Enough dinner for us all. Son and husband. I want to go back.

We make plans to return to the desert and stay in a cabin we found through a friend of a friend. When I think of her solitary life, I don't think of the fault line that runs beneath her. I'm too busy imagining the house with roadrunners in her sunlit yard. The warmth. The space. The time. I want to know how she makes a living doing what she loves while living in this place she loves. I imagine it's easier because she doesn't have a kid. But she's a writer too. And soon I'm asking the questions I actually have: Can I do what I love *and* give the people I love what they need? Does desire ever end?

On the darkest days, I think I'll never surprise myself again. I do the dishes, laundry, diapering. I settle into the obligations of love. I look around for something else to clean so I won't have to think. I end up with the taste of wet wool in my mouth.

I want the desert. I've always loved it. Maybe my lungs are low-functioning in high humidity. Or they just don't have the capacity to take in the air they've been given. Or maybe the desert ground is more honest, the way it visibly shifts beneath every step, acknowledging that it can take you to your knees. Such a risk makes me feel strangely alive. It fills with deference.

I have the same feeling when I'm on an airplane. I duck through the small door, and the wheels leave the tarmac, and although I pray for a brief moment to feel the earth again, to put my bare feet on the soil, it doesn't take long for the engines to vibrate their Novocain into my body. My head falls back. My palms turn up. The hum of the plane hums inside: If this plane goes down, there will be nothing I can do. I control nothing. Clouds. Radiation. Turbulence. Nothing is mine. The thought shades me. I forget myself. I enjoy the recycled air. I never want to land.

When I was still nursing our son, and felt the endless need of another person, I used to escape by putting my head on the pillow and pretending that I was on an undiscovered mountain, so far away that no one would ever find me. Ever. I lay down at the very top of the cold mountain and closed my eyes, listening to the silence of being perfectly alone. I stayed there as long as I could, wishing the time away without knowing that when you're a parent, the days are interminable but the years flash by and are gone.

Already, we're older. Our baby is three. I love him. And you. I love my life. But I keep imagining another in which I exit. I own nothing. I hold no lease or policy. Our son counts his fat fingers, and I count the days until the cactus will poke our shins. We'll call the trees Joshua, and they'll ask us for nothing. We won't worry that our son never sleeps. We will all stay up. Because: Stars.

They shine, but we won't see them this year. It turns out, we aren't going to the desert. We're having another baby.

We're pregnant and about to be jobless. Without health insurance.

It's possible that we're already spiraling toward destitution and brokenness—that we won't be able to stay together or love our way through this.

But for now, when we find out about the baby who has somehow happened even though we were trying *not* to have a baby and it seemed impossible that we would, we sit across from each other and stare—the deer in each other's headlights.

The pregnancy test makes a cross so faint that we quietly say, "Okay."

We say, "I don't know."

We take two more tests and both reveal the same faint symbol of yes, of more, of this too can happen.

Other people will say "accident," trying to nail down the unexpected. But it's the wrong word. There is no word. No thought. Every edge of every thing vibrates and is startled into a new kind of life. The lamp on the desk. My shirt cuff. The plus on the plastic, a plus one, a person who comes like a seismic thought, uncontrollable and uncontrolled into my head. Heart. Belly. Balloon. I enter the crisp air outside. I tremor over grass and dandelions, released into this life that is all surprise and shake, without pattern or want.

DEAR PHOENIX

Walla Walla, Washington
December 13, 2014

Dear Joaquin,

I was talking to a friend this evening as we drank something strong that her husband made for us to make us feel good—so good that we were talking about going to the movies. We two mothers, who work full-time and have lost the time we once had to make things, would make time to sit in a movie theater. Next Tuesday. (Maybe Bill Murray! We would happily watch Bill Murray do nothing more than chew gum.) We wanted to be IN the theater, IN the dark, with our hands IN popcorn, slathered in the butter that her husband claims to be the cause of all sickness in the world. During the $5 (!) matinee, I won't exist in that world. I'll slip out of this life where fathers and brothers die—this life of known death where we are mothers. I will slip away from my four-year-old son and my three-month-old daughter and into the lives onscreen. My worry will be for people who are not actually alive even though they will feel fully alive to me. No house of mine will burn down. No child of mine will fall. And no one will ask me for shit. No one will interrupt the internal thoughts I must keep quiet in order to make sure the milk glass is full again after it spills.

I'm going to the movies! I'm gonna hang my very existence on a screen of Bill.

He's like you with that crumpled smile, so lonely and sweet. So willing to be seen. He moves through his hurt.

"Have you heard of the new Pynchon movie?" my friend asked.

I'd had that drink (that something strong) that is still in me now, and I said, "Yes. Joaquin is in that." As if we're on a first-name basis.

"He's wonderful," she said. And it isn't just because she's an actor that I trust her perspective. It's that she always seems able to create. She's a brilliant mother interrupted. She wanted to make a play in which she speaks a monologue while holding her baby on stage. The baby would interrupt what she's making. Cry. Burp. Poop. My friend was going to transform this mother-rupture.

"Have you seen his movie that's like a documentary?" she asked.

"No," I said. "But it's weird that we're talking about it. Today, for no reason, I watched that Letterman interview he did. The one where he had a full beard and dark sunglasses.

"There's a moment when he asks about Dave's cut cuticle. He actually seems worried. It's like he just wants to talk about something that matters. But the camera zooms in on the blood, which prompts a forgettable joke and a jump to the commercial."

We took more sips of that something strong.

"I feel such tenderness for him," I said.

She nodded, and I realize now that what I want to say is I feel such tenderness *from* you.

I felt the same during the dance performance we saw tonight. Five women dressed in black danced without music. They moved to the sounds made by their own feet—a sound that patted along with their breath. They moved toward each other until they were sitting on the ground in a circle, their faces bent down to the stage. They started to hum the same note. They hummed into the circle they made and that hum reached into the audience with tiny vibrations like the tongues of snakes. Their torsos shot up and collectively embraced. Each body reached toward another and reached deep into me.

I wasn't alone in feeling. A brief wail rose from a woman in the audience. She stood up. A man followed her out.

The dancers let go of each other and stood at the edge of the stage. No longer humming. No longer touching. They held up their arms and began to lower them, slowly, so slowly, in unison. The motion was almost imperceptible. They didn't touch but moved together, their limbs made of twists, spindle, and reach. They looked like a set of Giacometti figures, those sculptures of the human body thinned out like branches, rough without leaves and still limber. Those naked winter trees walk with life.

The women lowered their arms in silence until their individual bodies formed a coherent gesture of opening to vulnerability. Of opening to loneliness and grief. Of perpetually opening a hand that reaches out to a hand that is not there.

This is the way I write this letter to you.

This is the way that you fill the frame.

You don't seem to fear the loneliness inside. You seem to rise up from the grief that loneliness affirms. You let it come.

All the best,
Kisha

P.S.
I've only written one letter like this before. (Eddie Vedder.) I didn't send it either. I kept it for myself.

P.P.S.
I thought about mailing this letter if only because I like to think of it held by the hand of one postal worker and another. I like to think that this letter will be trashed. I imagine it breaking down in a plastic trash bag. It doesn't seem like such a terrible end. The letter would rot with the coffee grounds and some orange peel, pits of cherries, and olives. The seeds that were once alive

will decay and eat the ink of this paper that was also once alive. Trapped in the future of that plastic bag, this letter will become the wet slop of an unread and unreadable past.

P.P.P.S.
This is how I wrote letters when I was a kid. Postscript after postscript. I always seem to have something more to say the minute I say goodbye.

P.P.P.P.S.
I tried to sleep, but I'm drinking water now. Trying to get out of this drunk feeling. Because there's something I'd like to ask, very clearly, without cream and Kahlua or vodka, or whatever it was that floated the ice: How do you keep going?

P.P.P.P.P.S.
I don't mean to make you my Ann Landers. I mean to find the creative act that initiates correspondence.

Walla Walla, Washington
December 14, 2014

Dear Joaquin,

Today, I believe in the clarity of my mind. It is bright and determined after writing to you through the night. I stayed up because I wanted to. I was awake for myself! Not to tend to a sick child or hungry child or any child. I woke up feeling connected to my ability. This morning, I lived in this fantasy and called it home.

I stepped outside to find the small town where I live covered in mist. A full bag of trash on the front porch shined. It soaked my shirt when I lifted it into the can. The lid slammed, and I flinched. When I opened my eyes, I saw by my foot a dead bird on the sidewalk. Feathers matched the concrete. Gray on gray. The bird might have vanished altogether if there hadn't been a small trace of blood on its beak.

That happened hours ago, but the image is crisp to me. The blood on the gray bird has filled my mind all day. I've watched it and waited, wondering if something will rise from it.

-Kisha

P.S.
The mythical phoenix carries such a heavy load. To live it has to rise from its own ashes. And it might be able to heal other people's wounds, but it has to cry to do it.

Portland, Oregon
December 22, 2014

Dear Joaquin,

My friend ran out of time to make her baby-interrupted monologue. Her baby started talking. These days she names the places
she wants to go. (Park. Library.) She has opinions of her own.
    My baby hasn't slept for nights. My toddler never sleeps.
We're traveling. I just want to sit alone in the quiet for days.
I have ten minutes. Then I have to feed the baby from my
exhausted body.
    I exist like a splayed hand: at my pinkie, the dinner I need to
make; at my middle finger, an idea; at my thumb, my children.
These fingers can't seem to work together. They grab nothing.
Or they write to you.
    But what does it mean to make a composition out of two fig-
ures without the second one?
    Finally. A question!
    Ten minutes is up.

    -k

Portland, Oregon
December 26, 2014

Dear Joaquin,

I read a quote this morning, written in large letters. It said: *There is no hope of achieving what I want, of expressing my vision of reality. I go on painting and sculpting because I am curious to know why I fail.* [*Giacometti*]

What's it like to be the kind of person who says this and *believes* it? Completely. Not the kind who says the word fail and:

1. Secretly hopes it won't happen;

2. Cries big, embarrassing cries; As embarrassing as this stream of uninteresting sentences for;

3. Who gives a fuck that I'm so sad about my failures;

4. Why do I cry? Why can't I look at my failure the way I look at a cut in my arm?

When I cut my arm, I feel like the cut has happened to someone else. I see the blood from a distance. And I *am* curious. I think: I made that blood. How?

When others get hurt, something else happens. Something weird. Another person's fall sends a Taser shock between my chest and pelvis. I actually hurt. Is this empathy? Or me assuming the intensity of another's pain? Even if the pain they feel isn't that bad, it stays on my mind. The cut gets covered by a capable Band-Aid, and I ask again: Are you okay? I keep reaching through language as if it will connect.

-k

P.S.
I keep thinking that nothing will be as interesting as the things I wrote before my creativity died. Which of course is not the death of creativity but the death of belief in the self.

P.P.S.
I enclose in this envelope a stone. It knows how to patiently survive.

Portland, Oregon
December 27, 2014

Dear Joaquin,

I started these letters to you before I knew that in your most recent movie you play a character who works as a letter writer. He composes letters on behalf of people he doesn't know and which he will send to people he doesn't know. The act of playing a character within a character—the act of being in the mind of someone who must then imagine being in the mind of someone else—is a nesting doll I don't care to crack. When I finally get around to watching this movie (next week? never?), I'm most interested in seeing how you pull this shit off. Over and over. You seem to trust yourself as much as you say you do. You talk about the work you want to *experience*, not the kind you want to make. You don't plan it out. You show up. You say, "You should not learn your lines, you should not hit your mark, and you should never follow your light. Find your light." Forget the light. You claim to start a scene without knowing where you're going because you know it won't really matter if you can't get there.

As a writer, I'm a moonwalker. I don't know what I'm doing, writes the poet Tomaž Šalamun.

What trust!

That kind of magic feels like eating a star to become one!

It's the same for me when I start, but it's harder now to trust. It seems that someone is always asking: what do you mean? Explain.

Exactly, I want to say. *What does it mean?????????????* [*Ashbery*]

There is no life in exposition! I'm after the enactment of the experience!

This is an argument of course. But I have no interest in arguments even as I make one.

Today I can't even argue with myself. I'm burned out. I keep watching television, or worse, YouTube videos. I pretend it's research. I don't know what I'm seeking, but I know I'm seeking. This will be useful! A flame will rise from my scattered attention! I will find a way to spark from the burned out when the burnout is the result of making one person and then another and making them out of such love. Such love has burned this soft house of a body down. I write out of the ashes. I write a letter to someone who will never read what I've written. I write a letter toward the absence of mind that is my mind.

-k

P.S.

The sculptor Giacometti once wrote a letter to the art historian Peter Selz: "You ask me about my artistic intentions . . . ," he wrote. "I do not know how to answer your question very well." What he says of sculpture, I say of the essay: It has "always been for me the means by which I render to myself an account of my vision of the outer world and particularly of the face and the human being in its entirety or, more simply, of my fellow-creatures and, particularly of those who for one reason or another are closest to me."

Portland, Oregon
December 28, 2014

Dear Joaquin,

The poet Tomaž Šalamun died yesterday. I didn't know him, but he always felt like a friend. His words rose from *ancient tanks, decapitated trees, wailing young widows, orphans in the windows.* [*Hayes*]

I heard him read once, and he moved into my head. I made for him a sunny room with wood floors. Sometimes I hear him walking around.

Now I'm trying to listen to a recording of him reading poems, but my baby interrupts me with her crying. She's usually so happy but still hungry and needs and needs.

I'll feed her a potato. Something to keep her dreaming.

. . .

She's quiet now. Tomaž reads:

"'To a Golem'
Lost in thought,
you came to watch me.
I'm like an olive branch—your face."

My daughter's crying again.

. . .

Now quiet. I think she's asleep.

"I hear the motion of soft nibs.
Smoke rises out of me.
I evaporate into you, tasting your
fruit, passer-by."

Crying again. More crying.
Me too.

. . .

I made a cradle out of my arms to hold her. She sleeps. I must hold her to keep her asleep. I must hold her new life in my arms to listen to the dead. I must accept what I can't make in order to listen for what I can.

> "I shuck the black, silky
> festive hall of your warm breath,
> the impermanence of your life."

-k

Walla Walla, Washington
February 10, 2015

Dear Joaquin,

I'm finally watching *Her*.

Before the movie starts, the black screen of my computer makes a mirror. For a moment, I can see myself, waiting to lose myself. The woman I see in that reflection is so calm. So open. Cheerful even. I'm in this state when the black screen becomes the word her, which becomes a close-up of you. Fuzzy moustache. Hazel eyes. Reading. You're reading a letter. You read until it's revealed that you aren't reading at all. You're speaking into a machine that "handwrites" your words onto letters of soft blue paper. You speak on behalf of someone who can't say what they mean.

I watch and get loose. I enter this story and feel close to the people in it. Why must I check out of my life to imagine being with others? *Am I a monster or is this what it means to be a person?* [*Lispector*]

In the end, you lay down "beside" the woman you love who is just an operating system inside a computer. Even though she's nowhere, she's leaving. She doesn't know where she's going, but she's going. She can't explain anything other than her willingness to escape into the feeling of ignorance. She needs distance from what she loves in order to see what's possible.

When you learn she's leaving you, you make vulnerability so beautifully visible. But that isn't what drops me back into the flow of mind that is my forgotten imagination. It isn't the you of your character, and it isn't the voice of the operating system you've fallen in love with. It's the fact that her voice is disembodied. Separated, an ash, it rises inside to release me. Like fire, it travels. Like language. Like a letter written to a beloved who stays unknown.

Yours,

k.

FACEBOOK

Not long after the seventh-inning-stretch, the five women in front of me appeared on the Jumbotron. Everyone in the baseball stadium looked up to see the women's faces made immense. One woman bleached a smile. Another bounced the gold hoops dangling from her ears. But it was the woman with the shining black hair who looked directly into a camera no one else could find. She blinked eyelashes as big as pterodactyls, flapping them in slow beats that made the seagulls turn toward this fantastic new bird. The gulls circled, as if preparing to dive. They would escape this common ballpark of shitty leftovers, squashed ketchup packets, and greasy paper bags to find that dream-life where fish leap into the mouth and no bird wants for a mate.

The woman with black hair held up her cell phone and took a picture of herself on the Jumbotron. She stopped smiling, but her eyes still laughed. They *seemed to promise a wild delight not found in life.* "*I know where it is,*" *they seemed to say.* "*I could show you!*" [*Cather*] Even from behind, her hair shined like a lake, glittering with the promise that if you kept watching, if you waited and were patient, all the rough waters would calm. You could look into those waters and see a face shining back at you. It would be the face of someone who wants to know you.

She leaned back against the blue, plastic chair, trapping her dark hair between the seat back and her body. With her cell phone held up to her face, she typed some kind of caption and waited, watching for the response that only a screen can give.

The comments came. She thumbed down the face of the screen, so flat and reflective, looking at all the things other people were doing, and which I could only imagine:

The baby is here! So fat and Happy!

At the beach. Another sunset!

A Puppy. Nine Puppies. Homeless Puppies! Want one?

The surprises scrolled past and jumped up inside, yelling, yes! yes! Puppies! You too can feel like you're a part of something even when you aren't!

This is our new house. Come inside.

The avocados are ripe on the tree.

Here was another beach. The next girlfriend in a blue thong. Another vacation. A private beach this time, in Brazil. A private concert in Ripton. A private viewing of Wyeth's most famous painting of a woman in a wheat field.

"Christina's World!"

No one can see her face. Her back is forever turned to those who look. Her hair catches the wheat light. She leans onto her hip. Her legs follow behind. It seems like she's reclining in the wheat, resting her weary body, but her torso twists as if preparing to stab the horizon. She looks ahead into the distance where something known only to her hides—some sustenance. (Love? Blueberries?) She isn't resting at all. Her thin arms propel her forward with hidden strength. She's reaching into that distance, crawling, seized by something there—out there—deep and unsaid. In the wheat. In the ear.

What is it?

What's out there?

Buried and hidden?

What's inside?

The woman in front of me typed another line. I inched closer. Too close! She shifted in her chair as if preparing to turn around. She could. Any second, she might yell, "What!?" into my face until I smelled the aspartame and mint of her gum.

But she didn't turn around. Her voice stayed inside as she returned to her screen, and I leaned back into myself, even as I kept watching and waiting. For what I didn't know. There was something about her. And it wasn't her plump air-kiss or her eyes, lined with the best that Loreal had to offer.

Suddenly, she pulled her hair free, releasing it from the small space between the chair and her back, sending it flying into my face where it atomized and became the air all around. I breathed in the alcohol of that ten-hour hold hairspray, and I welcomed its caustic shine. Her sharp glitter scattered me into an inaccessible region where there was *no more world*. There was *no world yet*. [*Blanchot*] Beneath the surface of the image, were the words. The words would go through my eyes, and I would hear them.

But I couldn't speak and be fascinated at the same time. I couldn't say glow or name its source. I had no names in my head or heart. No person was close by and no person in me. I was far away from the earth of people I love and who might love me.

I was accompanied by fascination. I was like a man who stares up at a woman who stares out into the distance. *His fascination is not with what he sees but with what he imagines it conceals—what he has placed there.* [*Brodsky*] I felt the comfort of having an answer without ever asking a question, the comfort of recognition without encounter.

Someone elbowed my arm. Did I see that? The game was getting good! The elbow belonged to my husband. Had he been there all along? Beside me? Yes. He was my husband, and the woman seated in front of me was a woman, isolated, looking out into the field.

The pitcher threw the ball to the batter who made contact with such perfect force that the ball came alive. All who watched as it soared toward the fence felt the arc of its possibility, as it did for us what we imagined we could never do, soaring beyond that impenetrable fence where the seagulls kept circling the Jumbotron screen, looking for someone who was no longer there.

GOLDEN GATE

O California. You hold as if you can be held. Not even the hummingbirds mind that I'm so close to the lavender. They hover three feet from my face, their bodies impossibly still between vibrating wings. The last time I felt this good, I held my newborn son for the first time. My nerves took root and made something good. Now, I sit in this place that isn't mine, sleepy in the sun. I smell eucalyptus and the nearby hills, blooming even though it's winter. Green. Constant green is the season of succulents, the olive tree, and the ice plants. Lettuce escapes the garden beds. I'm surrounded by green, and I'm green. But with life? Or envy? I can't think of beginnings without returning to my own. Even as the sun's abundance pulls me up, the ground pulls me down, like a plant, or the dying, or the dead. I grow heavy under its warmth. I'm not awake. I'm not thinking of lunch. I'm thinking of death, and so I'm thinking of my father.

———————

Golden Gate. Orange, white, and blue are the colors of vertigo. When I look up, an orange tower goes dizzy in passing clouds. I go with it. I can't tell which way is up. My hand finds the railing. I look down at my fingers to find them firm and pale against the bridge's International Orange, the color used on runways to mark the place for landing and takeoff.

I don't want to think about falling so I think, falling. I see my body moving to the edge, even as I think, stay away from the edge. The same thing happens when I ride a bike and see a stone ahead in the road. I tell myself, stay away from the stone, as my bike pops over it and throws me off balance. I continue on without falling, feeling smug that I wasn't hurt by the thing I meant to avoid.

In the distance, the second tower is not obscured by fog but by people. They cling to each other as they walk. Few speak. If they do, they shout. The wind is a loud constant that only changes velocity. Hats are lost. Jackets fly open. Bike bells ring out. A woman yells and points at the water as if seeing it for the first time. On the orange beam above her head is a blue and white sign. "Crises Counseling," it reads. "There is hope. Make the call. The consequences of jumping from this bridge are fatal and tragic."

A man stops his bike. He gets off and leans against the railing. He looks across the bay.

He's a regular man doing regular things, but I watch him. I try not to, so I imagine his leg stepping over the rail to jump like so many others who do the same. One person every two weeks.

Two seagulls rise in front of me and float above my head. Their wings bend into V's to catch the air. Their wings are just wings, but to me they look too much like broken legs. And just like that, I'm imagining again what I never actually saw. I'm seeing my father's body in the street, after he stepped away from the curb, away from his life, his wife and two young children, away from his son's third year and my fifth, away from everyone and everything, every back pain and spasm, every bill and commute, every manic and depressive episode, away from his bipolar disorder and into the path of an oncoming car.

It has been thirty years since he died. I'm far away from that time, on a bridge he never visited, and yet he comes to me through his death. He never comes into my life in any other way. It's how I know him. I have him like a recurring dream, but only when I'm awake. He comes at me like a palm spread in front of my face that says, look through this. Or maybe it's more accurate to say that his loss formed my eyelids. I see all life through his death.

The ordinary man doing ordinary things leans onto the rail. My hand floats up as if I could reach him in time.

What sadness my dad must have felt. What sadness I feel. His hurt has formed mine. But I suppose every human body is a history of death and its future.

The man gets on his bike and rides away. I'm dizzy with relief. I might be crying a little or maybe it's just the wind or the salt air, crusting the edges of my eyes. I look for the white gulls only to find that they've gone. The sky is the same color as the water in the bay is the blue of the eye passing by in the strangers. I grab the orange rail. I hold fast to the beams where people come to die.

I have a stable life. A good life. I'm not afraid I'll jump. I'm afraid of what I know: I'm a carrier of jumpers and their grief. I might be contagious. I carry the stranger who is my father just as I might carry the bipolar disorder that might pass through me and into my son. This fear leads to the deepest one I don't want to look at. It's suddenly so hard and clear. More than anything, I'm afraid that my son could ever feel that sad. That alone. I'm afraid he'll die before I do. I'm afraid that he would want to.

O Pacific. When I'm home in the winter, far inland and too far from the ocean, I dream of starfish. I know they're called sea stars, but when I was young I learned to call them starfish. While both names are beautiful, I refuse to let go of this word from my youth. It's a clear thing I hold in my mind, with bright orange arms that regenerate. A missing arm can grow back. A severed arm can grow a new body. I dream of starfish, forming new bodies out of absence in order to cling to the rough surfaces that would cut a normal person to shreds. The roughness is a harbor for the starfish and a comfort. The difficulty is a home. That is all. It's a dream, not an answer. When my son wakes up, I'll teach him to say starfish before teaching him the word snow.

EMPIRE BUILDER

Someone spoke of . . . Prŏgress.
"Oh!" said my father, "why do you pronounce the word like that? pray give the ō long."
[Tennyson]

What to make of a diminished thing
[Frost]

I forget the sound of the wheels grating against their track until the whistle blows, and I remember how far I wanted to go in this life. I ride this train named "Empire Builder" and settle into my sleeping car, where I'm given "J. Rogét American Champagne." After a bite of banana, the "champagne" fizzes into soapy layers until I feel the rapid birth of every bubble turn into a dying and quiet, pop and gone. It's so awful in my mouth. I want more.

We move at a fine pace until a wheel on our train cracks. It shakes one of the train cars so badly that an elderly man tells a woman it reminds him of the war. He doesn't say which one. He doesn't hear her when she tells him we'll have to stop and remove the car in order to keep going.

The train rumbles and slows. The engines cut. Power off.

In the unexpected stillness, I can hear the other people on the train with the intimacy usually reserved for private rooms. A man in the next sleeping berth coughs up his illness. A woman unzips her suitcase. A kid whispers, "How long we gotta wait here?" A bottle cap opens and the pills spill out.

"I don't know," says his mother.

In the night beyond the train, a single streetlight flickers yellow through the dark. An electronic sign reads 11:14 p.m. –17 degrees. Two dogs roam the street. A man runs beneath the trees. He isn't wearing a coat. I see the bare flesh of his arms, pumping forward until he disappears behind the only building in sight at the edge of this town, at the edge of this state of Montana in a country called The Reservation.

I know of this place, but I don't know it. I could say the name of this town, and I'll still be warm, inside of this train while the man runs through the freezing cold. A couple nearby complains about the stagnant air, and I'm silently wishing for more of that American champagne even though I know of a girl who froze to death south of here and wasn't found until spring.

"That's where they found her," a woman told me. This is how she showed me around. I was a visitor, just passing through. She pointed to a clumped shrub with her chin as if noting a road sign. "Over there."

I followed her gaze, wanting to hide my everything white, my everything suburban, my dead-end street, my father, dead too when I was five, my everything sad girl and Georgia, where the ground seemed only to vibrate with loss for me; ancestors and slaves, the wounded and terrified. I felt them wherever I went, under the surface of the soil and under the surface of my skin. I had to feel something else. I would become a new girl by coming to the elsewhere in my mind that was the home of light and dust and the sound of constant hooves and motion, propulsion, forward into the green. Into the sun. Westward I came. Westward I come. America *could* be the greatest poem. It would revise me.

The woman pointed in a new direction. "They found another man, there," she said. I listened to her like I was learning to speak. "Found him close to the place where another woman had an accident and lost her arm. There." Before she finished talking, she turned to point again. "Her dog got shot over there." She noted each loss and then moved on, popping between the death-landmarks without explanation. When she stopped, she turned to me. "Stay for a moment," she said. She turned and walked into the elementary school where she would make sure there was enough lunch for all the children to eat.

I stood very still, looking, trying to think about death this way. There is where the girl died, I told myself. There is where the man died. There is where the woman lost her arm. There. There.

This is what people used to say to soothe each other. There, there, I say, believing that I can learn how to speak of the grief I come from. I can learn to say names as if they are landmarks and not lineage, to live as if grief is a landmark best used for orientation.

But I can't escape the backstory I keep having to tell even though I'm sick of it. I'm sick with it. I'm infected by the sadness of the country I come from with all its sad mothers and suicide dads; I come from a long line of poor white southerners whose twins died and parents ignored them and who hung the tobacco to dry in barns, and they just barely survived. I come from Welsh and German immigrants and maybe a few French, and a tribe we call Mississippi Mound Builder and another called Cherokee. Somewhere, back in the way-back of my history, I come from this tribe that was forced to leave their land and died on the way. But not my ancestor. She didn't go that way. My great-great-grandmother escaped into the North Carolina hills by marrying a white man named Petree. Like the dish where little microbes leap without a clear destination and sometimes end up making something other than themselves.

I'm embarrassed by my desire to claim this grandmother. I'm like too many other white kids who claim the killed to speak of their own margins. I say Cherokee, and I'm all the other loud, white kids on the playground who holler, "Me too! I'm Cherokee too." We jump around like this means shit, but I'm still white. Taught Jesus. The Pledge of Allegiance. The words that promised grace and never delivered.

I stopped believing those words and moved to this part of the country. Montana filled me with an empty vastness I want to call spirit. Another ridiculous thing for a white girl to say. I say, "Spirit," and I'm read as Romantic, as romanticizing. But

I'm not a fucking Romantic. I am searching for a way to speak of the dead and the ills of this country that is mine and still make room to hear *so many good mouths in corners*. [*Revell*] I say spirit, and maybe I'm not a rabbit whose ears are blown. I feel my sad infestation and feel the bugs moving beneath the bark of the tree and the blood in me.

Even now, when it is −18 degrees outside. 11:30 p.m. The man is gone. The frozen girl is gone. *There have been too many* like her and too many like me, but I still cry when I hear the poem "America." [*Smoker*] I tell myself that I love the country. Not The Country.

I tell myself, it's okay to love the voice of Whitman.

I tell myself that the sound behind the voice of Whitman is the scratch of a wax record and not the sound of trains that come only to go.

I tell myself all of this, but I listen to a version of "America," that I found without struggle. I didn't even walk to the library to put on headphones and search for it in the presence of others. I stayed at my desk at home and searched the Internet, clicking through icons until I found a version that was a voiceover for a video of children doing backflips in fields and riding bareback on horses that kick up the dust from this land of possibility. A tattered flag waves between telephone wires. "Go Forth," it reads. "Levis."

This version of "America" is an advertisement for jeans. I know the comfort of that broken-in cotton and the way it feels to stand beneath fireworks that pop and burst into the dark emptiness. The voice of Whitman calls out, "grown, ungrown." Endure. I can't. I want to. "Strong, ample," the children's muscles flex, fair in the light. "Perennial with the Earth, with Freedom, Law, and Love." I wear these lines like a t-shirt, and outside it is −19 degrees. The man wanders back into view and stands under the streetlight. Not even his hands are in his pockets. He just stands there in a cold that circulates like suffering, without progressing.

I want to sit out this part of the journey. I return to the sleeping car and tuck myself in, just another American girl, soft in the middle and squishy with all the sweet promise that comes with white skin, middle class, clean hands, and the endless stories of how a girl can overcome any grief to make sure others don't suffer.

I grew up sad, but I grow into privilege. And look how I shine, America. America. I am come, America. I live in a land *crisscrossed with as many intersections as a leaf*, but I ride this train named Empire. [*Goedicke*] I don't have to do anything but arrive.

WHITE

I'm white at the conference called The Racial Imaginary, when I hear the poet and panelist Farid Matuk say, I want all the white people to paint white paint on their faces. This is the project of every white person.

Yes! I think. That's what I'll do. This is my project. The word project fills my mind like a solution. Or absolution. Immediately, I'm ashamed. I'm more naïve than I was as a kid with a new box of Crayolas and a blank piece of paper without any lines—nothing but white to mar and from which to create. Here is the project: How to expose whiteness? And not let it exist as a transparency—the film on the cream cheese.

I am white of a white dad and a white mom of white parents who even though they were poor were still white. Even when my mom was not yet my mom and wore her yellow dress to the picnic where a man told her to leave because of her suntan he called black, she was still white. Her father was still white, and so he could tell the bullying man to leave. Even with a father who died, I'm a white daughter. No matter the difficulty, I'm still white. This is the white face point to paint over every experience and dollar and car ride and shame. The bubble of white keeps me up no matter how much I hate it. I don't have to be racist to benefit from white supremacy even though my mom raised us to believe in love.

I believed in that love, but I didn't dare talk back to those in my extended family *who needed to believe themselves white*, and who said a word I'll never type or say again, not even in service of a story, because why should a word like that be in service to my white mind? [*Coates*] Why should I ever have cause to be anything other than in service to those who have reclaimed it?

I'm a grown woman who must bend her white face to the ground and look down to the white roots of the white tree of me. I know already these roots are as white as the white faces who say "all lives matter," believing they are affirming love only to affirm that they don't understand what people of color are talking about. I know how white they are and how white hot they make my shame.

I'm thinking of them, unaware that in doing so I've started the act of separating myself from whiteness rather than looking at the whiteness in me. I'm so busy backing away from my own complicity that I don't actually hear what the poet says at all. I don't hear him contextualize his next comment by describing an image from the movie *Dear White People*, of a white man in white face holding a gun to his head. I only hear him say that white people should point a gun at their heads and pull the trigger.

No! I think. Not that! Not violence. Not death. But I forget the word again. Already, I forget that the request is not for death. It is for the death of whiteness. Of white violence. I can't hear what he says because I'm thinking: I hear you!

I hear him! I say over dinner when telling my white friends about my white response. I ask the white question: What kind of solution is that? I say the white thing: He doesn't know me. I'm different.

I tell my white friends about sixth grade, when I was one of ten white kids in a school of 800. I was left out. I was threatened. And I'm still talking about this without remembering that I was still white. I was bruised; I was white. I was eleven; I was white. Twelve; White. Then I was high school white in a school half white as required by the Supreme Court that determined my school district was too segregated. The desegregation program bussed students of color to better-funded, white schools and called it "Minority to Majority." "M. to M." In a school that was half white or half black, depending on who interpreted the figures, I was still white.

I cared about numbers because I believed they were markers of the equity I craved. But I cared more for the boy who sat next to me in art class. He was funny and sweet. My friend. Kind and beautiful.

One day we were asked to draw each other. We had to look at each other. He turned his face to my white face. I don't remember any words. I remember his eyes on my eyes. I remember his thumb, quietly rising up to my face to touch my eyebrow. He moved his thumb across it, from inside to out. Then he did the same to the other eyebrow. I felt an intimacy I couldn't name but understood. His touch filled me with sense and made sense to me. It was a softness that made everything else disappear. When he lowered his thumb, we weren't embarrassed. We picked up our pencils and drew.

And look how I return to this moment to explain my version of white. I'm trying to complicate my own whiteness by thinking of this beautiful black man. Thinking of such love keeps me from the difficulty of thinking about the white faces.

I'm hiding again from the white boys at my school who rode around in an antique truck, orange and rusting. One morning, they blew into the parking lot, standing in the bed of the truck, hacking up some version of the rebel yell. It wasn't 1959. It was 1993. I was sixteen. White. I also had a car. I left the door open and crouched down behind it to hide, too afraid to move beyond the frame of its protection. And what I remember about that moment at the edge of the Atlanta suburbs, at 7:55 a.m., just before the school day would begin and we would sit in our desks, was that the boys were holding between their combined hands a confederate flag the size of that truck bed. It waved between them as they yelled sounds that were intelligible only as hate, and which shook the edges of their bowl haircuts and made me rage. In my mind, I jumped in front of their truck and had a lighter to burn that flag. But in reality, I stayed put. All I did was cry from my safe position. As quietly as I could.

The poet doesn't need to hear this shit from me.

But I don't yet understand that I haven't heard him. I hear myself again: I have an idea! I need to talk of white to white—to the white you who keeps saying "all lives matter," and the white you who keeps asking for someone to offer a solution to the "problem of race," and keeps waiting for the person who is not white to explain, at last, how to make it better and give guidance as if guidance is owed—the you who leans again on anyone who isn't white to fix the white that went wrong. The white you who called in to the radio talk show that was admiring Beyoncé's revolutionary song "Formation" in order to complain that you, a white woman, felt uncomfortable listening to it. Good, I think. Let us feel a discomfort that is continuous and never-ending. For *what we call history is perhaps a way of avoiding responsibility for what has happened, is happening, in time.* [*Baldwin*] This persistent trauma, this deep dread and dislocation, are the feelings the white self doesn't have to face to survive. And must face to destroy what is happening in time.

I'm talking as if I'm not one of you. But I am. Look how easily I make myself the authority. How easily I take up the posture of knowing what I'm talking about. *I'm the weapon I can't say no to.* [*Schlegel*]

Most days, my biggest worry is how to teach my young children how to safely cross the street. I wait for the orange hand to turn into a person walking. I wait for the signal to tell them we can cross together.

My son is five. My daughter is two and still in my arms, as she doesn't always remember to hold hands. We wait at the crossing. The hand is orange. "Stop," I say. "When the hand is orange, we stop." Repetition is good for teaching children how to live. Or is it only good for teaching them how to stay alive? "Stop. Wait for the white person." The moment I say, "white person," I'm sick and struggling to find a better way. I must correct myself before we can cross. "I mean the illuminated person," I say, only to have merged the idea of a white person with illumination. "I mean the person who lights up." Fuck, I think. Fuck. What's wrong with me?

I'm not aiming for political correctness. I'm trying to speak with an accuracy that might speak to the white problem. I'm trying to acknowledge that I just said this shit thing because I'm white.

When the figure appears above the crosswalk, no one moves. It's only then that I say to my children: "When the person appears, you can cross the street." I tell them to watch for cars that might come around the corner without warning. "Be aware," I tell them, "but know that when you see a person you should walk forward—toward that person. When you see the figure, you can safely cross."

But I failed to say what I should. I didn't tell them what they must hear: You are able to cross so safely because you are white. You are white children of white parents. You have done nothing, and already you've benefitted from your white faces. You're white and even though that shouldn't matter, it does. Because it does, we are responsible.

I repeat the lesson as if I've learned it. As if it's mine to give: The white face doesn't have to be racist to benefit from suffering. You must get yourself safely across this street, but you must know that it's made easier because you are white. And once you understand that, you must white-face. You must dismantle the very white world that you benefit from. You must declare your whiteness to destroy it. But have I learned?

No.

The night I misunderstand the poet's call for white-faced suicides, I have a dream. There's a gun. Cold against my temple. My finger is against a trigger. Because it's a dream I can see the white whole of my face and my finger all at once. I can see underneath to the blood. I wake up with the taste of metal in my mouth. My lip isn't bleeding, but I believe it is. I'm shaking.

For a long time, I took this dream as a lesson—a gift of the kind of discomfort I imagine a white person should feel. For three years I held on to this interpretation just as I held on to my idea of what had been said in that panel. I stood like a witness to my own white response.

But I didn't understand the dream; I didn't hear Farid. I heard the response of my own white mind and made that response the thing that most warranted attention. I made it supreme. I performed the action of exposing the white mind only to create a narrative that protects my version of it—that I'm different. And here is the white mind at work—the hard shell of it, made to protect white awareness as a form of authority.

I didn't understand any of this until I did what I should have done first. Listen to the poet. It took this essay's imminent publication for me to email Farid and ask if I remember things correctly.

I did not.

He describes all that he already described during the panel. He includes a copy of the image he referenced. It's from the movie *Dear White People*. A white man has covered his face in white paint. He grimaces, holding a gun to his head. Farid writes:

> As you might recall if you saw the film, *Dear White People* centers on an African-American film major, Samantha White, who also runs an opinion radio show at her university called "Dear White People." She's required to produce a short film as a final project in her film class. She produces a fantasy project that inverts the long history of slapstick, violence, and degradation that we see in blackface performances both on stage and in motion pictures. In this project the white folks wearing white face come upon some trauma they can't reconcile . . . and it throws some of them into fits of anguish and, as is depicted in the still that caught my interest, some of them even get close to committing suicide, though no suicides are ever depicted.
>
> . . . I was interested at the time in the way that whiteface on "white" skin might make whiteness seem less natural, less of a given, less of a stand-in for universal humanity.
>
> . . . My thinking about that image of white suicide came with some nuance: I don't want actual white bodies to actually kill themselves, I want, instead, 1) all of us implicated in whiteness to risk failing over and over again as we make whiteness visible as a construct, as we denaturalize it and 2) I want all of us to work toward de-centering whiteness in ways so radical that they may in fact leave us unrecognizable to ourselves, they may leave us undone (you can see there the metaphorical leap to "suicide").

That's the kind of "suicide" I'm interested in, the kind where we're so committed to love and justice that we stop being who we are in fundamental ways, which is a kind of "suicide."

TRUMP

September 23, 2015

I live in a warm house with strong walls and fresh paint in colors I like even though I didn't pick them. My bed is warm. My husband is warm, even as he says, "Donald Trump is scary."

It's too late to be thinking about Donald Trump, but the name plows his face into my head. His hair in permanent hackle. His skin the color of a marshmallow that came too close to fire.

"He just had a rally in Alabama. 30,000 people showed up." I look up from the book I'm reading, and what I read is lost to the fact. That many people came together for him.

30,000 people is the size of the town where I now live, and I still can't comprehend that number of bodies in one place. The number billows but has no shape. Like power.

I turn away from my confusion and back to the face I love. I watch my husband floss his teeth.

We are afraid of cavities.

At the dentist, they take x-rays to find any hidden decay. As a precaution, they put a heavy lead apron over my torso. And, for the first time in a lifetime of visits to the dentist, my neck warrants this kind of protection.

"This is the thyroid collar," the hygienist tells me. She Velcros it together to protect me from the x-ray beams that radiate parts of the body to expose what otherwise hides. It's thick enough to stand up on its own.

I feel its pressure against my neck, and I'm thinking of my friend's husband. He has throat cancer. Most mornings he takes in the radiation that will—we must believe, we must hope, we must say—clear the cancer from his throat. With each thought of the threat, we try to return to love.

He's the best at it. He attacks the cancer with humor and sincerity. "Upward. Onward," he says. I don't know how, but I want to follow his lead. Such thoughts are hard to trust when it's week four. He has a fever. He can't seem to eat. And so I'm thinking of his wife, my dear friend. I am holding her in my mind.

None of us are aware that this time next year the cancer will be gone. None of us are aware that he will be called a miracle. We only know the reality of this moment when we speak if only to expose our ignorance and acknowledge how little we know.

The hygienist finally removes the collar, taking down the protective border between my skin and the everyday radiation in the air.

"Trump wants to build a wall," my husband says.

"What's he afraid of?" I ask.

My husband flosses. He goes somewhere else in his head, far away into another corner of his mind.

I go to belief. I tell myself it will never happen. I put my head down. I turn out the lights, and we go to sleep.

SEPTEMBER 30, 2016

"I hate him," says my son who is six, and it's my fault that he loves public radio. When I mute the candidate's on-air tirade, we enter a silence my son can't stand. "I was listening to that," he says. "I want to hear it." It's a request I don't want to deny. I understand the desire to hear the language that seems to confirm what we know to be true. "Turn it back up," he says. I wait. I wait for the "please" I've taught him to use when making a demand. The moment spreads like dust. I do not move. He does not move. We stubborn two. I tilt my head. I squint. I smile a little.

"Please," he says.

I turn it back up. The story continues. The cold talk. It's catching. Here it comes.

"He's stupid." My son has always talked this way when he hears this man's voice. He has always known what meanness sounds like. He knows in his bones when words come from a desire to harm and not to communicate. But he's still a kid. He says what he wants, and he feels good when he coughs a mean thing even though he knows that when he speaks to hurt, he ends up by himself.

"I thought stupid was a bad word," I say.

He looks away from me.

I search for the words to talk to him about what's happening, but the only ones I find are a festering kind. They make me shudder.

"Say what you feel instead," I tell him. But he's already said what he feels. He feels hate.

Really, I want to ask him: Do you think love can trump hate? Is the Dalai Lama right when he says, "The more you are motivated by love, the more fearless and free your actions will be?" Isn't this what the mystics and great theologians and great figures of peace from Christ to the first tree that ever lifted its leaves to the sky urged us to do: stare down fear with your burning love?

What can I say when I don't believe that love will keep us safe? How can I talk about how much I hate this man without making more hate? Is such a thing possible? Does language still work? What language can disrupt the language of fear without repeating its error?

Or, to speak plainly, my son and I are trying to find something to call this man. We want to find the words that will represent how we feel without becoming like him. But we can't think of a name. We fail to speak beyond the language we've learned.

How then can we emancipate ourselves?

How then to liberate ourselves from Trump, "the liberator?" [*Butler*]

OCTOBER 1, 2016

Every time the presidential candidate belittles another person, the reporters are startled. They report as if this startling is the news.

I turn off the radio and turn my attention to the mouse that keeps making its way along the wall of the room in which I watch television to avoid my mind. The show goes on as the mouse runs from the closet to a grate in the wall where the heat used to come out. It doesn't anymore. The vents were moved long before we lived here. The grates are just for show. Their faux ironwork offers ample room for a mouse to slip through.

We worry about the mouse because it makes poop that might make us sick with the hantavirus. We tell ourselves it's a house mouse. House mice don't carry the deadly virus. It's okay. We'll catch it with a live trap and let it go in the park. But my husband has already set the death traps behind the television with a glob of peanut butter.

I watch for the mouse. A mouse is real. It's something I can think about. It has fur and a life. Its life complicates mine in a way that I can comprehend. I like the mouse. I might really like the mouse. And I want it to leave.

OCTOBER 3, 2016

I'm listening for the trap to spring when my friend calls.

His one-year-old son is hurt. He wants to know if I know anything about a drug called ketamine. "They'll use it to sedate him."

I know nothing. I'm on my computer, searching and finding nothing that will help, nothing that I can share with any sense of calm.

"Call your pediatrician," I tell him. "Then call me back."

He does. The pediatrician's triage nurse doesn't answer or he doesn't wait or who knows. It doesn't matter. They dosed the boy with ketamine and it's an hour later when he calls again to say that the stitches are in. The child did well but my friend fainted. He can't stop throwing up. Could I help?

Like us, they don't have family here. That is to say, we don't have family here other than each other.

I drive to his house and stay with his four-year-old daughter so his wife can join him at the hospital. I walk through the door so she can walk out. I feel so capable, so glad, to do what someone did for me when I was away and my husband's gall bladder attack sent him to the ER. Before he could go, he needed someone to watch our son. My husband called the neighbors who were so kind and good and full of love that my son still remembers that night as his first sleepover. The very best time.

It's 10:45 p.m. when I arrive. My friends' daughter is still awake.

"Mama Kisha is here," my friend tells her. This is what we call other parents, a term composed of my name and my promise, my hope, that this little girl will always know me as Mama Kisha, who loves her.

This is our actual life. This is language. This is the language that makes good what is good.

She puts her head down to sleep, and I sit on the couch in the silence, listening to the breeze move through the trees outside. A mouse runs along the edge of the wall.

OCTOBER 7, 2016

I'm watching movies again. Movies I don't care about. Tonight it's a movie called *Mockingjay*. The title speaks to my need. I want to have some kind of mockingbird sing the noun on my behalf—a mock—that which is performed as a form of demonstration.

I like this movie. It takes me out of myself even as it clarifies the feeling I have when I say the word citizen. I like the final lines, spoken to a baby by a woman whose last name is Everdeen. The sound of her name spells itself out in me as Ever-Dean, as in forever the leader: "I'll tell you how I survive it," she tells the baby. "I make a list in my head of all the good things I've seen someone do. Every little thing I can remember. It's like a game. I do it over and over. Gets a little tedious after all these years. But there are much worse games to play."

October 11, 2016
A good thing I've seen someone do:
+ A neighbor watched my son this afternoon. He went over to her house. They watched baseball.

October 12, 2016
A good thing:
+ My son was so excited that his sister pooped in the potty that he helped me make a chocolate "poop" cake to celebrate.

October 15, 2016
+ A little boy at my daughter's daycare brought Teacher Angel a gargantuan zucchini. And apple butter.

October 16, 2016
+

We had set the traps wrong. We fixed the error. There's no more mouse.

OCTOBER 17, 2016
+

OCTOBER 18, 2016
+

OCTOBER 19, 2016
+

OCTOBER 20, 2016
+

OCTOBER 21, 2016
+   I stop listening to the radio for good.

OCTOBER 24, 2016
+   I return to Anne Carson's *Antigonick*. I re-read her version
    of a story that has been told for 2,400 years. Before anyone
    knew the name Christ, they knew the name Antigone. They
    knew she screamed into the mouth of power and got buried
    alive.

OCTOBER 25, 2016
+   I return to the lines told slant. They lean into me.

    this reminds me of Samuel Beckett who described in a letter
    his own aspirations toward language
    "to bore hole after hole in it until what cowers behind it seeps
        through"
    [*Carson*]

OCTOBER 27, 2016
+ "You are so big! So biggie-big-big!" This is what I say to my growing daughter to let her know how much she is growing. She's almost three. I say it to make her laugh, which is the only way I know to respond to pride.

NOVEMBER 2
+ A little boy made a collage of stickers for my daughter's birthday.
+ She pressed the collage against her chest while stuttering a thank you. She's so my daughter. Her mouth wants to say the words while holding them close. It hurts me to hear her struggle until I decide her stutter is a form of agility—a willingness to reconsider. A refutation of certainty.

NOVEMBER 3
+ *it's not that we want to understand everything*
  or even to understand anything
  we want to understand something *else*
  [*Carson*]

NOVEMBER 4
+ A student made pumpkin bread and brought a loaf to share. This is the first year she'll vote. She's baking through the tension she feels. She lived in Texas and knows what a wall can do, the way it can render the night into a series of yellow lights that pulse in the distance. She brought a little blue bowl filled with warm butter and a knife and napkins. We sat outside and talked about Rita Dove. We talked about what it means to be denied a choice. In other words, we talked about rage. We talked about *the wild sorrow of someone who feels betrayed by the world she thought she knew.* [*Dove*]

NOVEMBER 6

+ My friend emailed today. My fierce friend. It's the first time I've heard from her since her recent stroke. She mostly writes with pictures because her left arm isn't working as it did before the stroke. She writes that her arm, which she has nicknamed, is lazy. For a moment, I live inside of her message. This moment of reading is so good to me. Her humor is so good to me. Through it, I see her suffering. Suffering is always complicated. Responding with grace is always a version of nuance.

NOVEMBER 8

+ Our neighbors make dinner and serve delicious beer at the party for election night. Within minutes we're applying our methods of living. The television clarifies nothing. We watch as if watching will make a difference. We speak as if our words haven't come too late.

7:15 PACIFIC STANDARD TIME

I'd rather be home watching a different show about massacre. *The Fall* this time. Season three. About a serial killer and the cop who finds him and holds him like Jesus in the snap-closed finale of season two.

No spoilers here. Just a clue that what's to come has already come. Just reality. Just another woman holding up a fragile man who destroyed women to feel worthy of being held.

7:20

My son, who is six, still only six, says at this party thrown tonight in honor of our nerves, "I want to shoot him." My husband catches the shot in his ear and leans close. "That is not ok."

I get involved. "You cannot say that."

I don't tell him what I really mean: You can't say that at this moment because we are imagining the holes in this body of a country. But it's worse than that, isn't it? His words extend from a language of hyperbole without any relationship to depth.

8:00 PM
We go home to wait.
  I stand at the kitchen counter, staring at a wall.
  "I think he's gonna need to be impeached," my husband says.
I finish his sentence in my mind with assassinated.
  What is the root of this word?

This is the oppressor's language

yet I need it to talk to you
[Rich]

8:16 PM
I hold my son's art project from school. The cotton balls rise up in an arch from the paper, held up in the middle by two stacked cotton balls. "I'm the only one that made it come up off the page," my son told me this afternoon.
  "It's beautiful," I said. "It has dimension."

8:17 PM
On his way to bed, my son asks who's winning. I warn him that his candidate might lose. "Not all is lost," I tell him. "We live in a democracy. And that means that one person can't hold all the power. Not even the president. If he wins, we'll make a plan of action. We'll find a way to make a difference. We'll find a way forward. But we won't say we are going to shoot him. We're better than that. We must be better than that."
  My son crosses his arms. His cheeks are so pink. "Let's just sack him." He's been reading *Harry Potter*. And I'm relieved. He doesn't echo the radio or some reality television show he's never even seen. He echoes the words from his favorite book.

8:20
This time tomorrow night I'll sit in an audience of a play whose speech I need to hear. Anne Carson's Antigone will scream over the dead brother she tries to bury in the earth of her own belief. Her country.

8:25
"I don't recognize this country," a few friends say, and I see how clearly I do. The rhetoric of this moment is the rhetoric that has percolated beneath the surface of life all of my life, intended to limit anyone beyond the limit of accepted form. I have known this form of the country to be my country all along.

9:02
This is happening. This has been happening.

9:41
After I watch Antigone scream, I'll only be able to think about the form of the scream. In making her screams, those fireworks of mourning, Antigone's voice pitches up to a sound that is almost a note. Layers of discord slip. I listen to her voice pitch between uncontrolled realms and the hold of a recognizable note. Can a scream, made to obscure all other sounds do nothing other than confirm its existence? Or can a scream become a song?

10:05
Tomorrow, my friend will contact everyone she knows. She'll ask them to leave the house at 5 p.m. Mountain Time to stand outside and scream.

10:09

Tomorrow, we will whisper our dismay to each other in public spaces. We'll speak in code, already afraid of who will hear us. Or we'll stay silent, afraid that words won't matter. It will take time for us to remember that we have an entire history of people who did, in whatever way they could, speak with clarity and scream with precision.

10:42

Tomorrow, reality will settle in along with my uncontrollable crying. It won't stop for the hours I must teach or the hours I must face my students, my students of color, my students who are undocumented, my writing students who still believe in language. I plan to write on the board: "I have lost my voice. What do we do when we feel we have lost our voice?" I will want to write this on the board but can't. Instruction requires exchange. And I don't own the day. My response can't limit theirs. Instead, my students arrive to find a handout I've placed on each of their desks, four pages of quotes that begin: *People are frightened of themselves.* [*Robinson*]

10:50

Tomorrow, my son will erase the monsters he drew on the whiteboard in my office, monsters defined by red eyes that would, he said, "melt your brain if you look at them for more than ten seconds." He'll erase all of them and draw instead a ship that looks like a plus sign. Inside of it he'll draw the two of us and write our names. Above the plus of his ship he'll draw a heart. He'll have so much to say that his words will exceed the size of his original heart. He'll keep drawing additional parts in order for all the words to fit. He will draw until there are four chambers big enough to hold these words: *Kischa u oywas will Di in mi hrt.* He will read it to me: "Kisha, you will always be in my heart."

10:53
Tomorrow, I'll cry like a person has died. This is before I realize that the grief I feel won't go away. This grief is my country.

10:55
Tomorrow, I'll remember that I'm related to women who agreed to this devastation. My aunt. Distant cousins. They looked at the face of hate and claimed that it alone would save them. These women are in me. But so are my ancients, grandmothers and greats who knew how to hold suffering in one hand and love in the other. They press the two together to sing the language of prayer. My mother. My literary mothers. Tomorrow, I will sit under a tree and listen for these women. I will beg them to let loose in me: In the right pinkie bone that types every : and the femur of fuck you. Please. Be the words in my body.

11:30
For now, for tonight, my only thought is this: suffering has always been the bone on which the flesh of a country hangs.

11:32
The next president is announced.

On television, the white woman next to the white man holds her hands to her cheeks and mouths

o my God.

Someone unseen holds her up on his shoulders but no one dares to look at his strain. Only her face is visible. Her bright blush fakes the sun-kissed look when, really, she's been here all day, under the false light of this arena.

o my Language.

This day can't end here.

This day can only end with a woman named Cixous. She is French. She moved here in me. I am her immigrant. I am working through the translation of being woman. I speak the

language once called hysteria—another strength read as illness—the danger-language that ravels and unravels. At once. To
be both. To and. To move BETWEEN< >ONE< >AND< >INTO
< >ANOTHER until *every word is the back of the hand that slaps
and the inside of the hand that holds. That cups.*

These words are in me, but I can't locate who said them.
I hear Judith Butler, but I can't confirm she's the origin. I am
ignorant. Through my ignorance, I abandon man's law of credit.
I locate my body of debt: none of my words are originally mine.
I learned them from everyone. Just as my body was born of a
series of bodies.

Let's return to the year before I'm born. 1976.

Let's return to the year we were all born.

Antigone is screaming in the foyer, and Anne Carson is
writing down her words on the bathroom stall, translating the
scream into song. Meanwhile, Hélène Cixous is with Medusa at
the mirror, laughing a new language as the toilet flushes inter-
mittently: *Woman must put herself into the text—as into the world
and into history—by her own movement.* [*Cixous*]

I move into the language of an erased body. Even when it
sickens to die to feed the soil, I return—not with hope—but
with fingers and mouth—to write *that good mother's milk*—the
white ink. [*Cixous*] I form words with my body and receive them
with my body, and it is this corporeal language that torments
the public. It snakes. It forms a woman's hair and kills me into
life.

This narrative isn't linear. It is inscribed. On my forehead. Come closer. Read what it says. This is how to *observe,
approach—to make love better, to invent.* [*Cixous*] Be vulnerable.
Enter the state into which we were all born—the only state
that can birth the blinking questions. Let us learn a language of
suffering to end suffering. Let us write in erasure to make the
absence known.

OIL

AN ERASURE OF GENESIS

In the beginning, the earth was without form. The face of the deep moved upon the face of the waters. Light divided from darkness, shall become light, is becoming light. The earth brought forth great whales, and every living creature of the earth made the earth over and over and over and over.

There went up a mist from the earth. Dust of the ground breathed into life, out of the ground, pleasant to the sight, in the midst of the garden. Knowledge of good and evil went out and parted and became the onyx river. Bone of bones, and flesh of flesh, taken out of one flesh, naked and not ashamed.

Eyes opened in the cool of the day. Hid amongst the trees, between Enmity and Grief, Impulse and Rule, the ground of lives, thorn and weed, sweat of nostrils. Bread. Return. From her you were taken and to soil you shall return.

Of the ground, a flaming sword turned every way to keep the way. In process of time, brought the fruit of the ground unto hot faces, downcast. "The portal in the field is Brother. Am I my brother's keeper?" Voice of blood, of brother of you, from the ground. The earth opened her mouth to blood, a fugitive and vagabond in the earth.

Upon the land, a city and tents and cattle; the father of the harp and organ; an instructor in brass and iron. All the days lived were generating and becoming all days. There were giants in the heart. The earth filled with pitch. The high hills were covered in nostril life.

A wind passed over the fountains of the deep. A raven went to and fro to see the face of the ground, but found no rest for the sole of her foot. An olive offered burnt offerings: "The ground's heart is from every living thing, seedtime and harvest, cold and heat, summer and winter, day and night—the fear of you—every moving meat, a green flesh. Life is blood."

The earth overspread with backward faces and not nakedness. Sons born after sons of the sons of the isles divided in their lands. Every one after his tongue, after their families, in their nations. Sons and sons in the city of–ite–ite–ite. The families of–ites spread abroad. In their countries, in their nations, the name of one was the earth divided.

Tongues after nations had brick, stone, and slime for mortar to build and make a name. Scatter upon the face of the earth. Nothing restrained them, which they imagined to do. Their language scattered upon the face of the earth. And the earth did scatter.

Out of country and house, a nation passed as land, as place, as oak. A mountain pitched west and east and called to the king of king, the king of the vale of the salt sea by the wilderness, in the vale, the king and king and king of four kings five.

By night, the valley of the earth delivered a thread that will not take. The young men eat the portion of mortals, "Fear not!

The stars seed the land. Inherit it. Take heifer and goat, a ram and turtledove and young pigeon. Divide them, each piece one against the other."

The birds came down upon carcasses. The sun was going down. A deep sleep fell, a horror of great darkness, for iniquity is not yet full. The sun was a smoking furnace, a burning lamp that passed between pieces.

From river unto river in the wilderness, the fountain said, "Affliction." The flesh fell . . . the flesh of the day . . . flesh of flesh . . .

Money appeared in the plains and sat in the tent door in the heat of the day. Eyes looked toward the ground, and said, "Pass not away. I pray. Rest under the tree. Hasten into the tent. Make three measures of fine meal. Knead and make cakes. Fetch a calf, tender and good, and dress it. Eat. Return. Old and well. Laugh within. Wax old. Have pleasure. Is anything too hard?"

Life, which is come and went, drew near, and said, "All is but dust and ash. Wilt the city."

At the gate, in the street, old and young people from every quarter call, "Shut the door." Under the shadow, pressed sore upon the door, the city is waxen before the face. Lingered the hand upon the hand. "Escape. Be consumed. Magnified."

"I cannot escape. This city is a little one. I have accepted this city. I cannot do anything."

That which grew beheld fear. "What has been done to us? Fear is this place and will slay. A thousand pieces of silver cover the eyes."

The burnt hand and knife went together to slay Fear, caught in a thicket by his horns.

Years of life died out of sight.

At the gate of the field, people bury the dead and the silver. The borders made possession of all that went in the gate. Country and Kin follow again. Give. Take. Be willing. Again. By the well of the city, the flocks and herds and silver and gold and camels and asses have given all. Words bow to eat and drink. After that, go away in the land named Fear.

Death sowed the year. The wells stopped and filled with earth. In the valley called Fear, eyes were dim. Weapons quiver and take near the smell of raiment, the smell of a field of dew and the fatness of the earth and corn and wine. Eaten words cry, with subtlety taken away: "What good shall life do? Take and make?"

The sun set on the earth, the seed, the dust. The families of the earth, awaked afraid. A great stone was upon the mouth. Flocks gathered and rolled the stone from the mouth.

The children, with great wrestling, called and found mandrakes in the field—rods of green poplar and hazel and chestnut tree. When the cattle were words taken away, the field said, "Change. Suffer. Hurt. The speckled shall be wages? The cattle bare speckled and the ringstraked shall be hire? Taken away? And given."

The rams leaped upon the cattle, speckled and grizzled. Sheep stole and fled over the river, toward the night. In the day, the drought consumed and the frost by night. Sleep departed from eyes. Fear had been the stone. A witness.

Fear called to night and early morning and sons and daughters and departed and returned and stayed. Fear, as the sand of the sea, which cannot be numbered, lodged that which came: ten foals, the fjord, the breaking of the day. The sun halted upon the children of sinew, upon the hollow of the thigh. Children over ground embraced and fell and kissed and wept. Eyes saw the tender flocks and herds with young.

Soft as cattle, the children in the land, pitched the city. The gate of the city circumcised the city. Fear called the ghost-gathered days. A veil wrapped an open face. Time thread into the night.

A vine budded. Blossoms shot forth ripe grapes. The grapes gave a basket of birds. By the river, came up seven well-flavored cows. Upon the brink, seven ears of corn, rank and good.

Seven thin ears sprung up after them. The seven thin ears devoured the seven full ears. Upon the bank of the river, seven other cows came up, poor and ill and ill did eat the fat. When they had eaten them up, it could not be known that they had eaten them; they were still ill-favored, as at the beginning—and the plenty forgotten.

The face of the earth waxed sore. With their faces to the earth, the naked let Fear commune with them. Their heart failed. They were afraid, saying, "Fear. Weep. Eat. Silver. Gold. Ground. City. Speak in ears, old and little dead. Eyes cannot pass the words a little food."

Fear, buried and dim, stretched, unstable as water, into the secret assembly, gathering blood and milk to bear a fruitful well whose branches run over the wall, the grieved, the arms, the hands, the shepherd, the deep, the breasts, the womb, the utmost bound of the everlasting hills, the crown of the head, wolf, the prey . . .

The field made a face to speak a sore lamentation for seven days, called into the land and the cave an unsent messenger—Fear—in place, thought, this day. Fear not speaking shall bring up the bones.

THE VEIL

In the years behind our years, there lived a woman who didn't need a wedding day to wear a veil. Julia Pastrana had a husband. He took her from town to town. He walked her from hotel to stage. He hid her marketable face from the public that had not yet paid. This was the configuration of his world. To go anywhere, she would have to cover up. She would have to wear a veil.

Under the veil, in every city, she passed through crowds made of eyes. Boys stopped slinging their pebbles. Men buttoned their topcoats closer to the neck. Women tried to gasp through the tight-laced corsets worn in London that year. 1857. They registered her difference. Her dark skin. Her thick eyebrows. The new moon dark of her eyes. The veil. It moved with the person it enclosed. Like wind in a sail, it moved with a hidden force, one that could move a body across oceans if charted by the stars.

Those who wanted to see beyond the veil would have to pay three shillings to get off on her face. They would have to come to the theater and commit to the act of watching her. They would have to wed their monster vision, refusing to say human. Woman.

This was a time of spectacle. Of P. T. Barnum and Human Zoos. Of "Miss Julia Pastrana," who stood on their stage so they could view the "Marvelous Hybrid," the posters had promised. The "Monkey Woman." The "Bear Woman." "From the jungle," said the pamphlets even though she was from the mountains of the Sierra Madre in Mexico, born to a tribe who saw the black beard covering her infant face and cried out *naualli*, wolf, shape-shifter, half-human.

Currency. Her uncle sold her to a traveling circus. The circus sold her to a governor. The governor made the rules of the household that kept her. He made her his maid and entertainment. Still, she learned to read. She learned to speak Spanish. And English. At twenty, she learned to run away.

On the road, she met a man on a horse. He rode high toward conquest. Mr. Rates. An American. He took her. He sold her to Mr. Lent, who married her to make sure she was never sold to anyone else again.

There would be no domesticity in the small hotel rooms. She was checked in and out. Her husband opened her private door to anyone who paid the extra fee. Only then was she told to remove the veil and let each paying man search the shining hair of the beard that hung from her chin.

Investigations of her beard led to her mouth, which she opened for each of them so they might try to catalog the absence of certain teeth, the presence of unexpected ones. "Breasts," one wrote. "She has the parts of a woman entire." Of her hair, the doctors said: "Opaque, straight, not Negroid but something else altogether." Something else. Something "animal. Hybrid. Baboon. Ourang Outang. Bear. Bear-Woman. The Misnomered. The Nondescript," as in that which has not yet been described.

When the curtain opened, Julia wore no veil. A single body constellated animal and human. The crowd didn't know how to see what they didn't know to see. She was a being for which there was no language. First came the desire to fit her into the little boxes of their minds. Then came the growing desire to do more than look—to touch her and touch that which could not be described. She might not recoil from this touch. She might hover closer, close enough to erase the gaze between them and expose to them the question they were too afraid to ask: Am I you?

She too wore small black shoes. She wore a velvet dress of her own making. With a "well-turned ankle," she danced the Highland Fling. She sang "The Last Rose of Summer," in a mezzo-soprano. She surprised them with her ability to speak. To speak English. To speak Spanish. She surprised them with her ability. Her 4' 6" body stood in for the conversation no one would have. By the end of the night, she had completed the impossible task: she stood in the space of their fear. And sang. She sang into the silence of being watched.

By Moscow she was pregnant. Julia's husband didn't let her walk outside at all. Still, she knew star-rise. She knew moon-rise. The moon was a fine-toothed dragon with a soft stone of a heart. It bit through the dark fog of every city, past the gray buildings, the charred edges of the chimneys, past the confines of every structure and toward this sister-star like so many others, whose *powers of body and mind have in the past been strangely wasted, dispersed, or forgotten*—whose *powers flash here and there like falling stars, and die sometimes before the world has rightly gauged their brightness.* [Du Bois]

She delivered a boy with a beard like hers and hair that radiated down his soft back. For thirty-five hours, she shared his life. She held him beneath *the star-children and the twinkling lights as they began to flash, and stilled with an even-song the unvoiced terror of life.* [Du Bois]

When the baby died, her husband sold tickets to her greatest suffering. Spectators came to look at Julia in her hospital bed, and still they did not see. Three days later she was dead. Her husband sold the body of the child and the body of Julia to a doctor who embalmed them. He stood them upright. He bolted their feet to parallel rods and enclosed them in a glass case.

Together, mother and son traveled for more than a hundred years, displayed around Europe and America and finally stashed in a Norwegian warehouse. There, a group of boys broke in and pulled off an arm they saw as mannequin. They lost the baby's body in another field of disfigurement from which it could not be recovered.

It took an artist to repatriate Julia and bury her in Sinaloa de Leyva, Mexico, under a tombstone that reads: *Artista.* Artist.

Inside the coffin are garments ceremonial to her tribe and a photograph of her child on her chest. Someone removed the bolts from her feet and placed them at the end of the casket. They closed the lid. They lifted the coffin onto a plane. It rose to take her home under a new moon.

That was a time that is here now.

When it is dark to us, the new moon doesn't hide behind the shadow of Earth as so many people believe. It hovers between the Earth and the sun. The side we can't see is illuminated. It's *being beautiful belongs*
to nothing. [Notley]

DOLLY

DOLLY: I'll probably look the same when I'm 100, 'cause I look more like a cartoon than anything else. I love to paint and powder. I love the . . . [trails off]. I have a look, and hopefully it'll always be my look.

TOM: Yeah. But I hope to God that you like the way you look when you go home and take it off.

D: Oh I *do!* I'm very comfortable with myself—

T: [interrupts] That there's the caricature . . .

D: Oh I'm not that scary—

T: [interrupts] . . . and there's the real you.

D: Yeah!

T: No! You're not scary!

D: The real me?! [laughs]

[Dolly Parton, interviewed on *The Late Late Show with Tom Snyder*]

Dolly Parton's childhood home is a structure from another time; the tin-roofed cabin has a small, front porch that welcomes strangers without any screens. Inside, dried goods fill the glass

133

Mason jars and handmade quilts cover the chairs. There's a single bed that slept the family of two parents and twelve siblings.

Of course, this isn't Dolly's real childhood home. This building is a replica, located in the Dollywood Amusement Park where gas stations and burger joints never aged beyond the 1950s. After the guests make their own candles and visit the blacksmith, they come to the "homeplace." A placard explains that Dolly's mother reproduced the interior. All that's missing is five-year-old Dolly Parton with a head of soft curls, looking up at the sunlight to sing the first song she ever wrote. It's about her corncob doll. "Little tiny tassel-top, I love you an awful lot." She stuck a tin can onto a broom handle and shoved the makeshift microphone into a crack in the porch. The dust rose up and glittered in the sun. She stood in that spotlight, dreaming of the woman she would become. That woman was out there. She was already singing inside.

Along the streets of small-town Tennessee, the Parton girls were known for their hourglass figures, but they were good girls. Not like that woman who walked through town every evening. She wore red high heels and stockings with a seam that ran up the backs of her calves. She touched the world with those red lacquered nails. Her peroxide blonde hair was the sun.

"She's beautiful," young Dolly told her mother.

"She's a tramp," her mom corrected.

But it was too late. In all the world of faces, Dolly had seen the face she wanted. And the body. Those whipped cream breasts. That fairy-tale hair. Dolly went home, took a handful of flour from the kitchen cupboard and spread it across her face. She stuck wet crepe paper onto her eyelids for eye shadow, crushed crayons into blush, and burned matches for eyeliner. She stole her first tube of red lipstick from the general store. She dotted her beauty mark with black so it wouldn't look like "a pimple." She piled her hair onto her head and bleached it bright. She thickened it into glorious waves by attaching more hair to the back of her head. She bought a full wig made of synthetic hair. She bought a wig of real hair. Then another. And another. She never left home without adding hair. She learned to go from shower to show in less than thirty minutes. She lost weight. She had her breasts augmented, her lips lined with collagen, and the crow's feet around her eyes filled with Botox. She had unwanted skin removed, a chin implant, facial fat grafting, and eyelid lifts.

Now, at age seventy-one, even the space between her eyes, that tender plain where tiny lines reveal feeling, does not move. Her face hovers between where it's been and where it's going. It lacks time's signature. The permanent pucker of her mouth and taut eyelids erase micro-expressions, those flashes of feeling just $1/15$th of a second long that happen uncontrollably when a person speaks or sings.

"I'm a doll," she tells one interviewer. He looks at her like a doll. She might be real.

He leans forward with the heightened awareness that stems from disbelief. He looks at her the way convalescing patients in Japan looked at a strange new nurse, introduced to help them.

This nurse folded her hands, mostly like regular hands, but something was off about her blink and the stillness of the skin near her nose. She wore a bobby pin to keep her hair out of her eyes, but those eyes didn't seem to smile when she smiled. Her face froze in some places and in others it repeated motion like the pendulum of a clock, a movement that resembles life but isn't quite alive. Her name was Sara. She was an Android. Her retinas were cameras. Her yawn revealed unstained back teeth. She was so close to human and so not, residing in a space the Japanese roboticist Masahiro Mori called the "Uncanny Valley." This land of ghosts and other ageless creatures seems like a place we've been to before, but it isn't the way we remember it. It is a land of constructions made to look natural.

"I'm real," Dolly says. "So I don't mind telling you I've had cosmetic surgery."

"What have you had done?" the interviewer asks. It's a question that gets as close as he can get to the real question that bubbles up inside: What's it like to preserve yourself this way? What is it that makes us care? "Why do we humans have such a feeling of strangeness?" Masahiro Mori wondered. "Is this necessary?"

Who cares if her skin looks like bread? It's *her* face! Her hair.
Her breasts. Her waist, cinched in with a lacquered belt. What
if she is only turning her body into *her* body?

Dolly laughs. Lists procedures. The interviewer relaxes.
Dolly smiles and makes another aphoristic quip in the style of
Southern girls who know how to direct your attention away
from the very thing you want to know. "I'd rather die on the
operating table than from my own bad looks," she laughs. "I look
at my boobs like they're show horses or show dogs. You've got
to keep them groomed." Dolly bubbles onward, floating somewhere between a down-home country song and that figment of
timelessness called fame. She stays a comfort *and* so strange, ours
and not ours, hers *and* not hers. "I'll never graduate from collagen," she says. Pop. Blink. Dimple. The uncanny Dolly smiles
again.

"You keep a wig by your bed in case there's an emergency
. . ." Ellen DeGeneres informs the talk-show crowd. The come-
dian turns to her guest. "Do you ever *not* wear makeup?"

"Well I do. But I would never go outside of the house . . .
Especially when I'm in California with all the earthquakes. I
always leave my makeup on at night." The audience breaks into
wild applause. "I DO*OO*! I leave a wig on a lamppost or somewhere nearby in case I have to be rushed out in the street and
the news people are there . . ."

"How long does it take you?"

"Not long . . ."

[interrupts] "Or do you have it down to a science?"

"Yeah . . . it's . . . I'm down to a science."

"Well, I feel like . . . you could be writing five songs in the
time it takes . . ."

"No. Not really. I'm pretty quick . . ."

[interrupts] "Ya know. I'm gonna help you out. I'm gonna
give you a gift so you don't have to waste time anymore."

Ellen pulls a latex mask with long eyelashes and perfect
makeup from a bag. The blonde wig is already attached.

Ellen starts laughing and the audience joins in, but it's Dolly
who laughs the loudest. Her voice reaches up, all the way up,

to that highest octave, that most beautifully eerie pitch of the human voice.

"I've already got mine," Dolly says. "You put it on!"

Ellen puts on the mask and pushes her breasts together and the preserved image replicates as if it will go on forever. Dolly reaches for the face. "Oh! You look great," she yells. "I love it! I love it!" Dolly runs her fingers along the smooth latex. Her voice is barely audible as she says, "That's what I want!" The crowd cheers. They gorge on the image. They refuse to sing its elegy.

Back at the homeplace, the teakettle waits to boil. The hearth is clean and empty. The table set for six. How comfortable it all seems, to be in this house made to look like a home. *Welcome*, says the home. And yet, there is no voice. No one lives here. The chairs aren't made to sit in. The table is set, but no one is cooking. No one will use that butter churn again. No one will eat the dried beans in the Mason jar. The plates won't hold hot potatoes. We've been invited to a meal no one is preparing. Everything waits as if something is about to begin, but it's already over. This is the house nostalgia made.

I step inside. Strangeness fills me as I approach the table and see the dust on every spoon. This nostalgia isn't even mine, but it makes me a girl again—a girl, dreaming of the woman I might be. I sit cross-legged in the clover, feeling all of the strangeness of being alive only to die.

If you had asked me, I wouldn't have said my girlhood dream was to be a "singer," or "star," but it was a glittering dream just the same. It always involved a kind of love.

Now the girl in me is grown. There's no way to touch the person I thought I would be. There's no way to find her, other than to think of the long-gone girl, dreaming of the future woman that isn't me. The desire to return to her time is the desire to return to that dream—the moment when I imagined the person I might become—a person who never really came alive. What an awful feeling. *Nostalgia*. It's *the very face of human misery, so blinded and wasted by its exhausting effort to ascend to the source of joy and innocence.* [*Camus*]

Why not let the girl go?

The flesh is about to fall off anyway. Even the siliconed body will break down. The chest will collapse.

The magpies are already gathering in the corner of the yard, waiting for what remains. They'll take the shiny things and the meat. The bell-bottom pantsuit and the rhinestone belt. The lavender eye shadow that shimmers and the larynx that sings.

Long gone, it's still singing. The sound of it is faint but rising. The rocking chair starts to move. The teakettle begins to boil. A sparkling girl stands on the front porch. The evening sun forms a single bleached spotlight into which she sings: "Tiny Tassel Top, I love you an awful lot," and then "Hard Candy Christmas." "Islands in the Stream." "I Will Always Love You." "Jolene."

"Jolene." The guitar notes staccato as if thumped. The bass line slips below the fiddle's slow harmonic pull. Dolly sings, "Your beauty is beyond compare." Her voice is a honey she knows how to pour. She hits the warble notes with the Appalachian yodel of her youth. To sing of beauty, she sings of time. "Your smile is like a breath of spring. Your voice is soft like summer rain."

On the rare occasion that she was asked about her music (1973) by a man, she called the rhythm of this song a "heavier up-to-date beat." She didn't write this song in the 4/4 "common time," denoted by a C that means *tempus perfectum*, or perfect time. She wrote "Jolene" in 2/2 time, noted with a symbol that has a line down its face: ₵. It is a time signature that means *tempus imperfectum diminutum*, diminished, imperfect time—cut time.

In this diminished, imperfect time, Dolly sings to the image of another woman with ivory skin and flaming hair and eyes of emerald green. She sings her way deep into the threat of this youth, in awe of the danger. "Jolene, Jolene . . ." She sings, knowing that, *beauty is nothing but the beginning of terror, that we are still able to bear, and we revere it so, because it calmly disdains to destroy us.* She sings into that bright hole. *Enraptures us. Comforts. And helps.* [*Rilke*]

DARTH VADER

It's evening when I watch my five-year-old battle with open abandon against the Empire. He stands on our front lawn, alone, swinging a bloated, red plastic baseball bat. It floats around him, glowing in the sun, just like a lightsaber should.

"Darth Vader," he says, "you are not my father. I will destroy you."

Sometimes my son accepts this paternity. Sometimes he loses his arm to Vader. Sometimes he cuts off Vader's arm.

He's Luke of course, and he is himself. He swings a bright light called a weapon.

For a long time, I suffered when I watched my son pretend to hurt another human being this way. My son understands Vader to be human. What had I done wrong to give him the impression that any person should be destroyed?

I watched and worried and let that worry obscure my memory. It took me too long to remember that I was this kind of child. I knew of villains. Bad guys. They could be named. Addressed. They could be vanquished.

"Vader," he says and takes a swing. But Vader never dies. It's as if my son is in a dream and wakes up before Vader can take the last breath that would end this vital relationship. And that's what it is. A relationship. Vader is a part of his life. He's a part of our lives. We talk about him at the dinner table. Vader doesn't eat. Or nap. Vader is not cute. He fights. He falls to the ground. My son laughs, only to raise his saber once more. Vader pops back up, ready for another battle.

My son damages his Darth in the yard only to come inside where he turns his Legos into weapons. He calls them blasters. They shoot black discs through the air. He has started shooting them at me.

"No thanks," I say. I start to remind him of the rule: don't shoot at anything with a heart. Nothing living. I've asked him to understand one thing: "When you pretend to hurt me, you actually hurt me."

I think he does his best, but it's very hard. His hands rise into a frighteningly natural position. He pinches his face in concentration, and in case we don't get it, he makes the sound of a laser when he shoots, a sound he has learned by watching *The Empire Strikes Back* and *A New Hope*. He takes his shot.

"When I grow up," he says, "I want to make *Star Wars* real."

I stare him down.

"*We* are real," I say.

He looks at me with annoyance. And pity. Don't I know this is just a game? Don't *I* know the rules? We are just fine. It's only pretend, lady. My son hasn't caught or killed Darth Vader at all. He doesn't want to. If the monsters ever get caught or catch us, the game will be over. We won't be able to outrun the monsters anymore.

He shoves the tip of his lightsaber into the dirt and makes a ditch that he fills with water from the hose. He digs down into the earth, making something only he can see.

My husband and I sit on the steps, watching him without being watchful, pleased that he is engaged in something that doesn't need our attention. For a moment, we talk as if no child is there because he isn't. He's in his own world. Beyond us.

Suddenly, he faces us. He takes a ready stance, holding the red bat in the air. The sun sets behind him. Its light fills his hair.

I can't see his face. He could be anyone, any child, a stranger, as everyone is a stranger, another person I don't know and will never know, living a life of his own, and shining in front of me his particular, vibrant, distant, ever-changing universe of a mind.

For a moment, I stop pretending to know what will keep him safe. I become a quiet telescope. I watch him move the light.

THE DALAI LAMA'S SHARKS

In the water, I'm meditation. With teeth. I'm human, but a leaf. I float in waters that aren't mine. This swimming pool belongs to my mother's friend. My body belongs to me, but it's not mine either. It grows without me. Adolescent. It hurts and then offers me the kindest feeling, as when a drop of cold water warms on my skin, or when a small leaf that has been floating on the skin of the water sticks to my arm. I don't notice it for a long time. The leaf rests on my arm, like any other arm, able to feel good and do good, be harmed and do harm. I float and feel expansive, not safe. Something internal, a kidney or the water that moves through my body, pulls me toward the bodies of water that move in the body of this earth. Only my head is heavy. My brain is in there. I struggle to keep my mouth and nose above the surface. I want to keep my face at the level of the sea. The sea speaks in feeling. If I open my ears, I'll hear it. I'll know my ears as ears. I'll be able to call my throat *the* throat. I feel the throat loosen. The tongue falls away from the roof of my mouth. The eyes soften and close. Or don't. Who cares. It doesn't matter. When a thought comes, welcome it. Then let it float away. The mind wanders and goes deeper inside. Inside of what? I feel pain behind my knee and turn to a place in my body that feels good. The earlobe. Where it meets my jaw. Does it meet my jaw? Is that my jaw? I never want to see my bones. I don't have heavy muscles. I float easily. The layers of fat that keep me warm in the winter buoy me in summer. My body eats and becomes food. *I am a carnivore, but a plant.* [Šalamun] Once a week, I photosynthesize in this pool. Then I dive. Nothing stops me. Even after I get a perm, and I'm told not to get it wet, I get it wet. The strands straighten back out. I've done a bad thing with my body, but I feel so good. I'm in water, with my hair loose behind me like tentacles. My legs fuse, and I dive through water tender with kindness and threat: of drowning; of rough concrete that skins the sole of my foot; of the sunburned, white boy who dives in to swim after me while our mothers spread their hips into the lounge chairs beneath the Georgia sun that stacks freckles onto their freckles. He comes after me. He comes for my feet and my legs and my body, which he wants for his own when my body is not yet my own. I don't know how to face his sad desire. I dive into the pool's deep end where a grate sucks down dirty water to filter out the floating skin cells and bacteria and chlorinate the water back to its false, tropical blue. I wrap my fingers around the grate and hold on tight. My lungs suffer. How long can they wait? I release one air bubble at a time, fighting the buoyancy of my body, its interminable desire to rise when I want to stay deep and hidden. I don't look to see if the boy's feet are dangling above. It doesn't matter. My body is beginning to inhale. I push off the concrete. My feet launch me upward with the power of a grown man, all muscle, all heat, all do not fuck with me. I'm going to surface in time to take the breath I need. I don't remember if the boy was there when I surfaced, but my body remembers—the dive let me escape. The response lodged in my body, in the muscles and little almonds of the brain called amygdalae. Whenever I'm afraid, they flood me with adrenaline and cortisol. I feel beyond what is seen and heard. When I'm afraid, my body surprises me like a poem. Even the Dalai Lama boards a transatlantic flight and gets a bolt from the blue—he fears most that he will survive the plane crash, and, having never learned to swim, will sink into the careless ocean and watch as his body is "enjoyed by a shark." He says the word shark and giggles. He laughs with his body made of meat. I hear his words, and I'm standing again on the edge of a boat, wearing a blue bikini for the first time, a color so absorbed by the sea and the Key West sky that I'm a cliché. My friend and I pay for the snorkel tour and ride the boat out to the coral reef. It's a slow, methodical ride. Waves kick the side of the boat. The air tastes of salt and sunscreen. The guide stops the engine. He hands us snorkels that fill our mouths with long, serrated tubes that turn every face into a creature without category. It takes two words to reveal who we are—a kenning kind of creature—so human-animal. "You," he says. "Jump in feet first." My feet are flippers. I flop to the edge of the boat. Clumsy at first, then capable. Look how my body learns! I stand at the lip of the deck and look down. Five large animals form a circle. "Jump there," he points to the hole between them. I can see their teeth. I spit out the snorkel. "Are they smiling?" I ask. He shrugs. "Barracuda." Until this moment, the word barracuda has only been a song to me, first released by a band called Heart. I only remember the chorus. "Ooooo barracuda. Oh yeah!" I can't seem to feel my fingers or arms. A shadow moves below the barracuda. "Was that a shark?" The guide doesn't look. "Sure." The shark passes again, with knives for fins, with its body made of cartilage instead of bone, bending like my human ear that will decompose when I die and be gone. The sun shines on the bait of my skin. "Someone else can go first," I say, shoving the snorkel back into my mouth so I won't have to answer for myself. I step away from the edge only to feel my body moving forward, without me, propelled by a single hand on my back, pushing me into the water. "Go," my friend says. My best friend. Lea Anne! She pushes me, and I fall. The flippers slap the surface of the water and slow my descent. I sink between the fangs of barracuda smiles, but what I really see is the shark in the near distance. A shadow shaped like a boneless cross. It grows. Closer. I surface. The strangers on the boat clap at me. "You're in now," yells my friend. That beautiful pusher. She pops in her snorkel and steps to the edge. I hold up my hand, but my snorkel swallows my warning. (Stop! Help! I'm afraid!) She jumps. The guide turns away. The others begin to drop their bodies off the side of the boat like lemons. Plop. Plop. We're all in, together now. My body bobs in the waves their bodies make. Through the distorted surface of the clear water, my legs curve unnaturally. My feet hang like worms from the hooks of my legs. They find their kicking muscles and take my body down. I dive into the water, past the circle of smiling barracudas, down and back. I'm a girl again. I'm a fish. I'm not thinking of the boy who chased me. My muscles hold that memory at the ready. My little almonds move me without thinking. Down I go through fear, a feeling that passes through a body with such speed that for a long time it was believed to be a contagious disease. While most of London died in 1655 from the plague, twenty-three died from pure fright. (Just believing a man was sick caused another to fall down dead.) Everyone was encouraged to practice calm even if they didn't feel it as they passed through a terminal landscape that passed through them. I pass through water, passed through by sharks. I pass through glades of teeth. I stop. I try to be still in a second as long as history. There's no stable orientation down here other than my body of connective tissue and ears and mouth and blood. My pores fill with the receptive jelly found in the shark's ampullae, those small pockmarks that register invisible electric fields made by the contracting muscles of nearby animals. All the jellies and starfish, the amoebas and all of Earth's first organisms that formed here before growing gills and fins and legs that walked onto land, all the birds before wings, the bears before legs. All beings formed deep in the body of the sea. Here, we first learned that fear is a form of intelligence. It's an ancient mouth in the brain that cries "Help!" Even when no one's around, we call out. This is no act of futility. It's a reminder that we believe in love—that someone out there loves you enough to listen for your call. Maybe god. Maybe mother. Maybe god. Here's life again in the form of thought. Help! Here's the shark, vibrating death with her teeth. The shark swims toward me only to pitch down. The shadow-cross of its body sinks away from me, into the dark. I swim up to the light. My body surges to the surface. My mouth spits out the snorkel to fill each patient lung with air. My body turns belly up like a palm to the sun. I move with the ripples. If anyone were to fly over in a plane, they wouldn't see me here. They would see a glint on the wave. A broken shell. A stomach with wings. Ancient. A single thought, reaching back to the beginning, when I shared this ocean with you.

LIBERACE AND
THE ASH TREE

In the children's backyard, the ash tree is a celebrity. It sparkles with sap. Its branches sign a dark autograph into the clouds. The children can't stand still. They dig around roots and climb. They drag out jackknives and carve their initials into the bark. When night falls, and they must go inside, the children cut down a limb and bring it into the house. Their mother stuffs it into a vase. They stare at the large leaves and only then do they notice the white buds about to bloom. They stare into the flowers as if this will make them open.

In the next room, their mother is playing a record of a bobbing piano tune that is a hit this week in 1950. She hums along as if her bones are made of piano keys. By the time she serves dinner, she can't sit still. Her hair is up, her lipstick red. Her skirt kisses her calves. She scoops the pudding into bowls as a car horn sounds. She closes the door and is gone.

At the concert hall, she joins a thousand Midwestern wives. The lights dim. The curtains open. The spotlight reveals a shining piano, and then he enters. Stage left. Dipping his prematurely gray pompadour to their uplifted cheeks, their breasts.

For them, he wears a blue Norwegian shadow fox cape and a King Neptune costume made of pearls and seashells gathered from the open ocean where bottlenose dolphins rub genitals to say hello and male seahorses have the babies. For the finale, he wears a tuxedo embroidered in diamonds that spell out his name: *Liberace*.

He plays one sparkling tune and another until the curtains close and it's over.

He had been the perfect man. Tender. Humorous. He would never gob a girl with kisses. He would always treat his mother well.

The fans wanted more.

They sent him love letters seven thousand times a week and made marriage proposals forty-eight times a month. They came by the thousands to airports of his arrival and fainted at the site of him.

"He makes us feel good all over," one said.

"He is the impeccable man we would like our sons and husbands to be," said another.

"He is just like a divine figure . . . so far apart from anything that is worldly or bad."

Again and again, Liberace held his bedazzled fingers in the air and waved his light onto the crowd. He was mythic. He was their Cosmic Adam, and they were his Eve. He waved as they waved, until the men of the press noticed Liberace's "soft, well-manicured hands."

"Did Liberace enjoy sewing over sports as a child," they asked.

"NO!" replied his lawyer.

No. Liberace assured.

If they did not believe him they could watch the women in pursuit. "If they were waiting for Jayne Mansfield," Liberace said, "it would show that there was something wrong with the sex life of the world."

But, "Liberace," the press asked, "do *you* lead a normal sex life?"

By the end of summer 1954, one publication had the answer: "Don't Call Him Mister." He lived a secret life, they said, and to a male lover once gave a cigarette case inscribed, "To my darling, whom the world forbids me to live with, and without whom I cannot live . . ."

Two weeks later Liberace announced his plans to marry the cabaret dancer Joanne Rio. He hadn't proposed exactly, but had an "agreement" to marry her in a year, once his concert schedule slowed, and once he had given his betrothed "the full Catholic treatment."

In the meantime, he would have this former neighbor and proposed wife type up her adoration to share with the public. With Liberace's publicist as her editor, she told the world, "He brings me orchids. He lights my cigarettes, and he opens doors."

The fans already knew their man would treat a woman this way. Liberace's love of Rio was real. The fans fell into despair.

A woman from Milwaukee wrote to her Liberace, "I lost out again. I love you too much. I can't write no more. I am crying too hard."

A sixty-six-year-old widow from Saint Paul, Minnesota, wrote, "I feel sorry for your mother. The adoration you give her will have to be shared."

From Colfax, Iowa, "Why, oh why didn't you wait for me? I'm only eleven but I practice the piano every day."

From Boston: "Don't forget Joe DiMaggio and the promises she made to him!"

New Orleans: "Will she love you like we do?"

Liberace would not be deterred from his love. "Anyone who sacrifices his personal life to the public is very foolish," he said. "I'm sure that the public wouldn't want that. Actually, women adore a lot of male performers who are married."

The fans begged him to understand.

From Gardena, California: "Your appeal is the fact you're single."

Detroit: "How can you think of marriage? You belong to us."

Finally, he heard them. He asked his publicist to break up with Miss Rio.

The magazines returned to their question, "Is he, or ain't he?"

For a brief time, the ash tree was a little bit famous for making the Earth. If the ash had still been famous in the time of Hollywood reporters, the news would have been about secret flowers. Reporters would have revealed that ash flowers aren't what they seem. They can have two anthers *and* an ovary. They look female, but act male. Or they look male and are female.

If the ash were human, the humans would want an answer.

"What do we call you?"

What? The tree would say, *What?!*

"What are you?"

The May 1957 headline of *Hush Hush* magazine asked: "IS LIB-
ERACE A MAN? If not, what?"

But the columnist William Conner, pen-named "Cassandra," had already figured Liberace out. It was everyone else he
couldn't understand. "[Liberace] is the summit of sex—Mascu-
line, Feminine, and Neuter. Everything that He, She, and It can
ever want . . . [a] luminous, quivering, giggling, fruit-flavored,
mincing, ice-covered heap of mother love . . . there must be
something wrong with us that our teenagers longing for sex and
our middle-aged matrons fed up with sex alike should fall for
such a sugary mountain of jingling claptrap."

When Liberace sued "Cassandra" for libel, the courts confirmed that Liberace wasn't a homosexual. He swore under oath
that he was "against the practice because it offends convention
and offends society." For the self-proclaimed "one-man Disney-
land," perception was freedom, and "manhood and Freedom,"
he said, "are life itself."

By the 1970s Liberace was playing Caesar's Palace in a pair of red, white, and blue mini shorts with jeweled knee socks and a matching handbag. He collected cars and covered them in rhinestones and glitter. With each Vegas show, he slipped into something "more fabulous," to give the fans the man they wanted. And when the show was done, he returned to his home or hotel where he kept his male lover in secret and hired a plastic surgeon to make his lover's face look more like his own.

By the 1980s, *all were true to their icon, and they knew what to do.* [*Shimoda*] During his final stage performance at Radio City Music Hall in November 1986, the fans kept applauding as he stepped offstage between numbers to inhale oxygen from a machine. They told themselves he was so thin because of his new watermelon diet; they told each other he would go home to Palm Springs for a bit of rest.

And here is where the myth hits its limit, for it has already broken down. The Liberace Museum closed in 2010. All the feather boas and star-spangled shoes reside in storage. Everyone knows Liberace didn't lose weight because of watermelon. He had AIDS. He returned to California and soon, he needed help to walk. A friend put Liberace's feet onto his own feet in order to walk him from the private chapel once blessed by a Catholic bishop especially for him and into a large bed where Liberace could curl up and watch videos of "The Golden Girls."

By February he was in and out of consciousness. His nurse removed the rings from his fingers. She laid a string of plain rosary beads in his hands.

He died just before spring, when trees make the world anew, and the ash flowers clump together and become what they will become.

Don't be afraid. There they go.

SHADOW TEXTS

Jesus

DAVID BROMWICH AND MATTHEW BEVIS

David Bromwich has suggested that when Ashbery refers to "you," he "means only himself, farther in," which I take to mean that the poet's paying of his addresses is a way for him to retreat into isolation and inwardness. But perhaps "you" is not "only" that, for he is also discerning—or yearning for—an echo of himself in others.

"It Wants to Go to Bed with Us," *Harper's Magazine*, June 5, 2017.

TOMAŽ ŠALAMUN

Why do questions pile up like bailiffs

"The Cross," *Plume Magazine*, trans. by Michael Thomas Taren.

Bin Laden

HEBREWS 10:19–20

Therefore, brethren, since we have confidence to enter the sanctuary by the blood of Jesus, by the new and living way

which he opened for us through the curtain, that is, through
his flesh . . .

The Navarre Bible, 2003.

ETEL ADNAN

When old friends hurry to join the carnage
When the victors' eyes become live shells
When clergymen pick up the hammer and crucify

"XXXIX," *The Arab Apocalypse*, 1989.

Mother Mary

FERNANDO PESSOA

We never know self-realization.
We are two abysses—a well staring at the sky.

The Book of Disquiet, trans. by Richard Zenith, 2002.

SAMANTHA HUNT

When I became a mom, no one ever said, "Hey, you made a
death. You made your children's deaths." Meanwhile, I could
think of little else.

"On the Unspoken Terrors of Being a New Mother," Interview with
The New Yorker, May 15, 2017.

BARTHOLOMEW

And as they all were doubtful and pondered the matter to and
fro, Bartholomew came to her with a cheerful countenance and
said: You who are highly favored, tabernacle of the Most High,
unblemished, we, all the apostles ask you, but they have sent
me to you. Tell us how you conceived the incomprehensible, or
how you carried him who cannot be carried or how you bore so
much greatness.

New Testament Apocrypha, Volume 1, ed. by Wilhelm
Schneemelcher and Robert McLachlan Wilson, 1991.

MARY

But Mary said to them, "Ask me not concerning this mystery. If I should begin to tell you, fire will issue forth out of my mouth and consume all the world." But they continued the more to ask her.

> The Apocryphal New Testament, ed. by J. K. Elliott, 1993.

GERARD MANLEY HOPKINS

Comforter, where, where is your comforting?
Mary, mother of us, where is your relief?

> "No worst, there is none. Pitched past pitch of grief," *Gerard Manley Hopkins: Poems and Prose*, 1985.

Ozzy Osbourne

ROLAND BARTHES

The Photograph belongs to that class of laminated objects whose two leaves cannot be separated without destroying them both: the windowpane and the landscape, and why not: Good and Evil, desire and its object: dualities we can conceive but not perceive (I didn't yet know that this stubbornness of the Referent in always being there would produce the essence I was looking for).

> *Camera Lucida: Reflections on Photography*, trans. By Richard Howard, 2010.

Dick, about Your Heart,

JOHANN WOLFGANG VON GOETHE

There may be a difference . . . between seeing and seeing . . . The eyes of the spirit have to work in perpetual living connexion [*sic*] with those of the body, for one otherwise risks seeing past a thing.

> *Goethe's Way of Science: A Phenomenology of Nature*, ed. by David Seamon and Arthur Zajonc, 1998.

Since its intention is to portray rather than explain, [morphology] draws as little as possible on the other sciences ancillary to biology, although it ignores neither the relationships of force and place in physics nor the relationships of element and compound in chemistry.

"Observation on Morphology in General," *Scientific Studies*, ed. and trans. by Douglas Miller, 1988.

Wild Things Are
MAURICE SENDAK

The night Max wore his wolf suit and made mischief of one kind . . . and another . . .

Where the Wild Things Are, 1963.

ST. THOMAS AQUINAS

On the contrary, Augustine says: "There can be no doubt that there is no cause for fear save the loss of what we love, when we possess it, or the failure to obtain what we hope for." Therefore all fear is caused by our loving something: and consequently love is the cause of fear.

"Whether love is the cause of fear?" *The Summa Theologica*, trans. by Fathers of the English Dominican Province, 1947.

MAURICE SENDAK

. . . Max said "BE STILL!" and tamed them with the magic trick of staring into all their yellow eyes without blinking . . .

———

But the wild things cried, "Oh please don't go—we'll eat you up—we love you so!"

———

. . . but Max stepped into his private boat and waved good-bye . . .

Where the Wild Things Are, 1963.

JOHN ASHBERY

A mirage, but permanent. We must first trick the idea
Into being, then dismantle it
"Flowering Death," *Poetry*, July, 1979.

MAURICE SENDAK

. . . and sailed back over a year and in and out of weeks and
through a day . . . and into the night of his very own room . . .
Where the Wild Things Are, 1963.

Dear Phoenix

GIACOMETTI

There is no hope of achieving what I want, of expressing my
vision of reality. I go on painting and sculpting because I am
curious to know why I fail.
quoted by Morris Grossman in his book *Art and Morality*, 2014.

JOHN ASHBERY

What does it mean?????????????
quoted by Matthew Bevis in "It Wants to Go to Bed with Us,"
Harper's Magazine, June 5, 2017.

TERRANCE HAYES

Bemusedly [Tomaž] said, "America is a wonderful place to be a
poet. There are so many publishers, so many poets." In a bubble over his head I saw ancient tanks, decapitated trees, wailing
young widows, orphans in the windows of Eastern Europe. But
I'd been drinking, I could have imagined it. The bar was loud.
Tomaž did not preach, he did not frown. He seemed only to
telepathically ask me to reconsider my position.
"Stars Will Fall on Your Head: Tributes to Tomaž," *Real Pants*,
January 8, 2015.

CLARICE LISPECTOR

Forgive me if I add something more about myself since my
identity is not very clear, and when I write I am surprised to find

that I possess a destiny. Who has not asked himself at some time or other: am I a monster or is this what it means to be a person?
The Hour of the Star, trans. José Olympio, 1977.

Facebook
WILLA CATHER

Her eyes, when they laughed for a moment into one's own, seemed to promise a wild delight that he has not found in life. "I know where it is," they seemed to say, "I could show you!"
A Lost Lady, 2003.

MAURICE BLANCHOT

To write is to arrange language under fascination and, through language, in language, remain in contact with the absolute milieu, where the thing becomes an image again, where the image, which had been allusion to a figure, becomes an allusion to what is without figure, and having been a form sketched on absence, becomes the unformed presence of that absence, the opaque and empty opening on what is when there is no more world, when there is no world yet.
"The Essential Solitude," *The Gaze of Orpheus and Other Literary Essays*, trans. Lydia Davis, 1981.

JOSEPH BRODSKY

His fascination is not with what he sees but with what he imagines it conceals—what he has placed there.
On Grief and Reason, 1995.

Empire Builder
HALLAM TENNYSON REMEMBERING ALFRED LORD TENNYSON

Someone spoke of Dīplŏmăcy and Prŏgress. "Oh!" said my father, "why do you pronounce the word like that? pray give the ō long."
Alfred Lord Tennyson: A Memoir by His Son, 1898.

ROBERT FROST

The bird would cease and be as other birds
But that he knows in singing not to sing.
The question that he frames in all but words
Is what to make of a diminished thing.
"The Oven Bird," *Mountain Interval*, 1916.

DONALD REVELL

There are so many good mouths in corners, such sirens.
And I have no trouble speaking as they speak
now that the sky is clear and the dark mist
of police and animal noise has rolled on.
I am not with you. I hate no government.
I hate only those with no eyes for the weather.
"The Siege of the City of Gorky," *The Gaza of Winter: Poems*, 1988.

M. L. SMOKER

There have been too many just like them
and I have no way to fix these things.
"Another Attempt at Rescue," *Another Attempt at Rescue*, 2005.

PATRICIA GOEDICKE

The palms of our hands are crisscrossed
With as many intersections as a leaf.
"The Tongues We Speak," *The Tongues We Speak*, 1989.

White

I'm indebted to Farid Matuk, the poet who inspired this essay.

TA-NEHISI COATES

For the men who needed to believe themselves white, the bodies were the key to a social club, and the right to break the bodies was the mark of civilization.
"Letter to My Son," *The Atlantic*, July 4, 2015.

JAMES BALDWIN

We both have produced, all of us have produced, a system of reality which we cannot in any way whatever control; what we call history is perhaps a way of avoiding responsibility for what has happened, is happening, in time.

A Rap on Race, a conversation with Margaret Mead, 1971.

ROB SCHLEGEL

I'm the weapon I can't say no to.

"White Silence," Black & White & Read Exhibition, Cannon Gallery of Art, 2015.

Trump

JUDITH BUTLER

How then to liberate ourselves from Trump, "the liberator?"

Verso Blog interview, December 29, 2016.

ANNE CARSON

"one of my earliest memories," wrote John Ashbery in *New York* magazine 1980,
"is of trying to peel off the wallpaper in my room,
not out of animosity
but because it seemed there must be something fascinating

behind its galleons and globes and telescopes"
this reminds me of Samuel Beckett who described in a letter
his own aspirations toward language
"to bore hole after hole in it until what cowers behind it seeps
through"
dear Antigone: you also are someone keeping faith

———

dear Antigone:
your name in Greek means something like "against birth" or
"instead of being born"
what is there instead of being born?
it's not that we want to understand everything

or even to understand anything
we want to understand *something else*
    "the task of the translator of antigone" *Antigonick*, 2012.

RITA DOVE

The amount of vitriol in Helen Vendler's review betrays an agenda beyond aesthetics. As a result, she not only loses her grasp on the facts, but her language, admired in the past for its theoretical elegance, snarls and grouses, sidles and roars as it lurches from example to counterexample, misreading intent again and again. Whether propelled by academic outrage or the wild sorrow of someone who feels betrayed by the world she thought she knew—how sad to witness a formidable intelligence ravished in such a clumsy performance.

    "Defending an Anthology," *The New York Review of Books*, December 22, 2011.

ADRIENNE RICH

knowledge of the oppressor
this is the oppressor's language

yet I need it to talk to you
    "The Burning of Paper Instead of Children," *The Will to Change*, 1971.

MARILYNNE ROBINSON

People are frightened of themselves. It's like Freud saying that the best thing is to have no sensation at all, as if we're supposed to live painlessly and unconsciously in the world. I have a much different view.

    A 2008 quote posted on *The Paris Review Blog*, November 9, 2016.

HÉLÈNE CIXOUS

Woman must write her self: must write about women and bring women to writing, from which they have been driven away as violently as from their bodies—for the same reasons, by the same law, with the same fatal goal. Woman must put herself into the text—as into the world and into history—by her own movement.

———

There is always in her at least a little of that good mother's milk. She writes in white ink.

———

I've seen them, those who will be neither dupe nor domestic, those who will not fear the risk of being a woman; will not fear any risk, any desire, any space still unexplored in themselves, among themselves and others or anywhere else. They do not fetishize, they do not deny, they do not hate. They observe, they approach, they try to see the other woman, the child, the lover—not to strengthen their own narcissism or verify the solidity or weakness of the master, but to make love better, to invent.

"The Laugh of the Medusa," *Signs*, trans. by Keith Cohen and Paula Cohen, 1976.

Oil
HEBREW INTERLINEAR BIBLE (OT)

The Veil
W. E. B. DU BOIS

This, then, is the end of his striving: to be a co-worker in the kingdom of culture, to escape both death and isolation, to husband and use his best powers and his latent genius. These powers of body and mind have in the past been strangely wasted, dispersed, or forgotten. The shadow of a mighty Negro past flits through the tale of Ethiopia the Shadowy and of Egypt the Sphinx. Through history, the powers of single black men flash here and there like falling stars, and die sometimes before the world has rightly gauged their brightness.

———

Within the Veil was he born, said I; and there within shall he live,—a Negro and a Negro's son. Holding in that little head—

ah, bitterly!—he unbowed pride of a hunted race, clinging with
that tiny dimpled hand—ah, wearily!—to a hope not hopeless
but unhopeful, and seeing with those bright wondering eyes
that peer into my soul a land whose freedom is to us a mockery
and whose liberty a lie. I saw the shadow of the Veil as it passed
over my baby, I saw the cold city towering above the blood-
red land. I held my face beside his little cheek, showed him the
star-children and the twinkling lights as they began to flash,
and stilled with an even-song the unvoiced terror of my life.
The Souls of Black Folk, 1903.

ALICE NOTLEY
   your being beautiful belongs
      to nothing
   I don't believe they should
      praise you
   but I seem to believe they
      should
   somehow let you go
      "At Night the States," *A Grave of Light*, 2006.

Dolly
ALBERT CAMUS
   They are literally consumed by nostalgia; and this emotion,
   which people imagine to be so distinguished, then reveals its
   true face, the very face of human misery, so blinded and wasted
   by its exhausting effort to ascend to the source of joy and
   innocence.
      "Balthus," *Writers on Artists*, trans. by Jean Stewart, 1949.

RANIER MARIA RILKE
   For beauty is nothing but
   the beginning of terror, that we are still able to bear,
   and we revere it so, because it calmly disdains
   to destroy us. Every Angel is terror.

———

Is it a meaningless story how once, in the grieving for Linos,
first music ventured to penetrate arid rigidity,
so that, in startled space, which an almost godlike youth
suddenly left forever, the emptiness first felt
the quivering that now enraptures us, and comforts, and helps.
   The Duino Elegies, trans. by A. S. Kline, 2004.

The Dalai Lama's Sharks

TOMAŽ ŠALAMUN

   I am a carnivore, but a plant.
   I am God and man in one.
   I'm a chrysalis. Mankind grows out of me.
      "The Fish," *lyrikline*, trans. by Michael Biggins.

Liberace and the Ash Tree

BRANDON SHIMODA

   All were true to their icon, and they knew what to do.
      Brandon and I can't locate where he said this. Of it, he decided,
      "Maybe it truly IS a shadow-text, with the body removed . . ."

ACKNOWLEDGMENTS

This book extends from years of study and friendship with writers whose time, care, and intelligence have shaped me. At the University of Montana, Phil Condon, Neva Hassanein, Kim Todd, and Annick Smith allowed me to begin, as did Kevin Canty and Judy Blunt. Melissa Kwasny and Patricia Goedicke taught me to listen to the line. David James Duncan showed me how to believe. Lois Welch, Ginny Merriam, and Ripley Hugo guided me during the 10:20 Club. Natalie Peeterse and Mandy Smoker Broaddus shared their fierce, poetic hearts. Chris Dombrowski handed me a copy of *The Next American Essay*, introducing me to more of my literary kin. Joanna Klink said, Go. Find them!

The University of Iowa's Nonfiction Writing Program gifted me three years to write and be confused and keep writing. Robin Hemley's kind responses encouraged early drafts of the essays in this book and helped me refine later ones. David Hamilton cheered on "Wild Things Are," and Alexander Chee urged me to keep erasing Genesis. Honor Moore reminded me to enjoy it all. Joy Castro asked me to do a blind contour drawing of someone difficult. John D'Agata read my essays aloud to me, and through his voice I heard my own. Susan Lohafer's written comments on my essays are essays that continue to fuel my creative life.

Early on and ever since, Steven Church and Dinty Moore generously championed my work. Angela Pelster-Wiebe, Sandra Allen, Lucas Mann, alea adigweme, and Stephanie Elizondo Griest read with a love I keep with me to keep going. Chris Martin gave me the chance to read the first of these essays during a tornado warning. Nick Twemlow published the first, signaling that such a thing was possible. Kristen Radtke deserves buckets of flowers for seeing this book as a book, even before it was. The word fear would have appeared 172 times had it not been for Ariel Lewiton's keen editorial eye and generous friendship.

Inara Verzemnieks, whose insightful and unflinching love of the essay matches her boundless friendship, did more than encourage. She showed me how to keep writing no matter what—and how to warm any room with a paint color called seahorse. Lina María Ferreira Cabeza-Vanegas clarified that I write in translation; because of her, this book became a book. Amy Schleunes wrote with me until we didn't feel so alone. Brandon Shimoda's emails are the essays I strive to write. Sharma Shields has supported my work from the beginning, as she does for so many writers of the great literary scablands. Her grace and wit is my guide. My thanks to Rawaan Alkhatib for making hearts with teeth. And to Dave Schulz for making those hearts the right size. Thank you, Jessica Cerullo for showing me how to turn a scream into a song. The writers Crissie McMullan and Jeremy Smith remind me how to keep writing *and* keep living. I'm so thankful for your sustaining love and intelligence.

Whitman College gave me the chance to teach while protecting my time as a creative person. My amazing colleagues in the English Department believed in me and this book, supporting me to finish it. Sharon Alker's kind questions allowed me to fill in vital gaps in this collection.

I wouldn't have been able to start a full-time job while finishing this book while parenting without knowing that Angel

Camacho was caring for my children and showing them another side of love in my absence.

My agent Julie Stevenson stayed on the publication rollercoaster with me. And kept me buckled in. Her love of words and humans alike keeps me hopeful.

Thank you to everyone at The Ohio State University Press. Thank you David Lazar and Patrick Madden. Thank you Kristen Elias Rowley for sending an email that said yes.

Thank you Lewellyns and Schlegels for being my family—for being sure of me even when I wasn't. Thank you Bob and Peggy Schlegel, whose continued interest in my writing echoes their immense love.

My poet-husband Rob Schlegel was a first reader and last. Thank you for your honesty, your friendship, and your willingness to be with me in the Heartland—and the Blues.

Hey kids. Thanks for your curiosity. Thanks for letting me call you mine.

Thanks mom, for, you know, everything.

Thank you, reader.

Similar versions of these essays appeared in the following journals. My immense thanks to the editors: "Darth Vader" *Tin House Blog*; "Dolly" *StoryQuarterly*; "Dick, about Your Heart," *Anomaly* (formerly *Drunken Boat*); "Oil" *Conjunctions*; "Gun" *Talking River*; "Empire Builder" *Kenyon Review Online*; "The Veil" *Marry a Monster* and Whitman College's *Global Studies Anthology*; "Liberace and the Ash Tree" *The Iowa Review*.

This book was made possible because of support from the University of Montana, the University of Iowa, Whitman College, and an Artist Trust Grant for Artist Projects.

21ST CENTURY ESSAYS
David Lazar and Patrick Madden, Series Editors

This series from Mad Creek Books is a vehicle to discover, publish, and promote some of the most daring, ingenious, and artistic nonfiction. This is the first and only major series that announces its focus on the essay—a genre whose plasticity, timelessness, popularity, and centrality to nonfiction writing make it especially important in the field of nonfiction literature. In addition to publishing the most interesting and innovative books of essays by American writers, the series publishes extraordinary international essayists and reprint works by neglected or forgotten essayists, voices that deserve to be heard, revived, and reprised. The series is a major addition to the possibilities of contemporary literary nonfiction, focusing on that central, frequently chimerical, and invariably supple form: The Essay.